Coach Wisdom

Volume II

The Secrets of 21 Successful Coaches

DIVYA LV JEGASUNDARAM

SNEHAL R. SINGH

ISBN-13: 978-1-7335836-7-1

Do you want to be in the next, "Coach Wisdom"?

Go to www.coachwisdombooks.com to find out how.

PRAISE FOR VOLUME I

5.0 out of 5 stars "Gentle Reassurance"

I am on my way to my own coaching business, finishing up training at this time. This book was refreshing to read because a majority of it was very supportive and spoke to some of my insecurities in this new venture. I think it's easy to find a lot of advice out there and a lot of "you should do this". While this book did have a bit of that, it had a lot of much more gentle reassurance. I don't so much appreciate the forceful advice that leaves you overwhelmed and discouraged, so this book was very helpful and fun to read.

5.0 out of 5 stars "Great book!"

From reading just a few of the chapters, I felt energized and inspired. The wisdom in the book is life changing and motivating. Any coach starting out or wanting to level up, would benefit greatly from reading it! Great book!

5.0 out of 5 stars "This book is a treasure! "

This book is a treasure. I guess I could browse through this and feel better any day that I am confused and feel stagnant in life. When Matt Gagnon says, *"living with a courageous heart"* and later brings out how people choose to be vulnerable, I could totally relate. Snehal's perspective *"Getting coached is about investing in yourself"* invokes a whole new dimension in my mind ...Got to read this peacefully on my kindle, over and over again, wonderful companion for my flights.

**5.0 out of 5 stars *"Coach Wisdom"* - Brilliantly Conceived -
*Delivered with Depth and Simplicity***

Congrats to Divya and Snehal for delivering the intimate heart to heart colloquy of coaching experiences and essentials in such a cohesive and simple manner. "*Coach Wisdom*" is a must read and a 'speaking tree' for all the aspiring coaches as well as for coaches already in practice. If you are looking for a 'thought provoking' 'inquisitive' 'simple to understand' and 'real life journey of coaches' you have to really add the "*Coach Wisdom*" book to your collection. Congrats Divya & Snehal for your inspiration via *Coach Wisdom*.

5.0 out of 5 stars Wisdom Galore

Perhaps it may be the first time that 21 Successful Coaches have shared their experience of their coaching journey including trials and tribulations and the joy finally achieved. The 21 Chapters are 'Pearls of Wisdom'. Going through the book has cleared many myths associated with coaching. Subtle points have been brought forward, which were not part of the Coaching curriculum. In my opinion this book certainly qualifies to be a 'Go-to' book for new coaches. I have benefitted immensely. The book is in the genre of 'What they don't teach you in Harvard'. My compliments to Divya and Snehal.

CONTENTS

ACKNOWLEDGEMENTS

WOW! Another year just flew by! On January 15th 2019, we launched Coach Wisdom Volume 1, and in 4 days it hit bestseller in multiple countries and categories. It's an understatement to say that we were ecstatic. Whilst hitting bestseller was a dream, our true sense of fulfillment arose from knowing that Coach Wisdom was reaching the masses and creating an impact way beyond what we had envisioned.

For those new readers to the Coach Wisdom series, the idea was born during a casual conversation in which we were talking about how, as coaching lecturers, we see so many people taking the time to get certified and yet many didn't seem to be able to do much with it post certification. This was often because they just didn't know how to proceed. As practicing coaches, we began recollecting our own journeys and agreed, in hindsight, that if we had a book giving us some ideas of the next steps, tips, industry do's and don'ts or best practices, it would have been hugely beneficial.

We had always imagined Coach Wisdom to be a book for Coaches by Coaches. In all honesty what we were not prepared for was that it would also be read, endorsed and enjoyed by entrepreneurs, leaders in organizations and many embarking upon their own personal development journeys.

So here we are. Exactly a year later, barely catching our breaths launching volume 2!!! It is with great pride that we present to you not just our 21 Coach Authors but also an entire bonus section dedicated to helping you create and sustain your businesses from all angles.

As with Volume 1, countless hours, days and months have gone into the planning and execution of Volume 2. Even though we had the experience of the first book, it certainly didn't make this one any easier to compile and complete. Amongst our many moments of laughter, exhaustion and sheer excitement we certainly experienced those moments of fear, doubt and frustration that reared their ugly heads from time to time.

Through what has been an amazing journey, we do have a few people whom we would love to thank and express our appreciation for their ongoing support, encouragement, motivation, feedback and cheerleading.

Firstly, thank you God for Your Grace and Blessings in providing us a platform on which we have been able to share and serve in the knowledge that we have gained as coaches. To our husbands, thank you for encouraging our creative, intuitive, crazy sides to just be. Thank you to our parents and immediate loved ones for being our excited cheerleaders in all that we do.

Thank you once again to Dr. Randin Brons, someone we both consider to be the father of coaching. If it hadn't been for your experience, your fabulous material from which we both became Certified Coaches and your enthusiastic energy for the Coaching profession, we would not have been so inspired and motivated to follow in your footsteps.

Thank you to all our fellow authors who have shown such commitment and dedication to adhering to deadlines, being graceful in accepting changes to your chapters and for the sheer excitement you have expressed in accompanying us on this journey.

Thank you to John Mattone and Marshall Goldsmith for your ongoing support in our Coach Wisdom dream. The support from both of you has kept us motivated to keep working towards making this dream a reality and striving to create this humble offering to the profession of Coaching.

Finally, we once again offer our heartfelt gratitude to our dear editor Vimala Vadivale. You did it again!! With your attitude; patience; knowledge; sense of humour; candid feedback and willingness to be part of our team you have given us immense happiness and pride in the finished product Coach Wisdom Volume 2. You graciously and tirelessly worked to meet our deadlines with a smile and we thank you sincerely for this.

For all the special mentions made here and to the readers and supporters of Coach Wisdom, none of this would be possible if it weren't for you. Once again it is with deep gratitude and humility that we sincerely thank each and every one of you for accompanying us on this literary ride!

So au revoir…. Till Volume 3!!!

Divya & Snehal ☺

FOREWORD
-JOHN MATTONE

THE WORLD'S #1 AUTHORITY ON INTELLIGENT LEADERSHIP AND BESTSELLING AUTHOR OF THE INTELLIGENT LEADER (2019).

What a great honor it is for me to write the Foreword to Coach Wisdom Volume 2. Congratulations to Divya and Snehal for having the big vision to help global coaches bring greater value to their clients—through the creation and publication of their enormously successful bestseller, *Coach Wisdom Volume 1.*

Due to the success of this book and the massive need that exists among global coaches—to constantly "raise their game" in how they position, sell and execute their coaching services to ensure they really provide value and ROI to clients who are more sophisticated and savvy than ever—Divya and Snehal have compiled *Coach Wisdom Volume 2.*

Like Volume 1, this book is a must-read for every global coach. *Coach Wisdom* will empower you to go beyond your certifications by learning from some of the top coaches in the world who deliver powerful and practical advice that will help you think bigger about the work you do as a coach and help you create actionable plans and steps that you will never learn in a certification program. Through the stories, experiences and anecdotes from these outstanding coaches you will gain insights and "insider" tips as if you were having a fireside chat with one another that will ignite your heart, mind and soul about the work you do as a coach and how you do it.

Coach Wisdom in many respects is the ideal handbook and guide for aspiring, new, even seasoned coaches. *"There isn't a coach in the world who cannot get better."* We owe it to our clients and to ourselves to commit to getting better and being better, every day. The one thing I see in the "best of the best" coaches is the mindset of quiet confidence and conviction combined with humility and vulnerability. As a coach, it is your responsibility and obligation to create that "special place" where your clients can learn this themselves, however this will never happen if you the coach don't embrace, internalize and role model these tenets.

Coaches, let's use the wisdom in this book to CHANGE THE WORLD!

PREFACE
BY STELLA LACEY- KATZ

A s we allow ourselves to open up to our most authentic and vulnerable personal journey in life and the inspiration to fulfillment and infinite realms of possibilities, I invite you to read this book of profound insights from a series of world renowned Coaches and best-selling Authors.

Throughout this book you will find yourself stretching past your own personal narratives, how to become prolific in your own unique beauty in this world, and how to transcend this energy through fulfillment, while you are on your own path to become more for others.

The unique span of intrinsic Authors in this book will undoubtedly help you gain insight and impose clear direction towards the energy's and ideas that will set the path of that which lights your soul on fire.

This fire, in my opinion will have you intuitively creating your own, very personable energy signature. This energy signature is what the world is needing from you, that has the capability for you to be drawn to create the impact which will inspire and evoke many lives towards greatness, to which your own future personal legacy will leave a trademark of infinity.

The knowledge of our lives, experiences, education and diversity is vital in how it relates to what brings us joy and fulfillment and how to incite the action we need therein to ask ourselves this one simple question, "Are we living in our purpose and ON purpose?".

Once we realize what the boundaries are that hold us back from our purpose, combined with energetic passion and with a desire to attack those fears head on, ANYTHING really is POSSIBLE!

This book is invaluable in helping you discover tangible ideas to help you become anything or anyone you ever dreamed could be possible for yourself, therefore others.

Thank You

Stella Lacey-Katz

Mentor Motivational Speaker Founding Member of the Les Brown Maximum Achievement Team Life Transformation Specialist Health and Wellness Coach Fitness Enthusiast

Instagram: Stellabratelifewithme

1

How Coaches Steal from Clients, And Why You Do Not Want to Be One of Them

BY STEVEN H. KIGES CMC

You may find the title of this chapter a bit odd; it may even have raised some curiosity? If it did, I am glad. Let me explain with a short story. About twenty-five years ago, I was a partner in a mid-size software company called Mercedes Integrated Technologies. I had a business partner, who was very wealthy. In our city, there is a private school where wealthy families would send their children. Now this school had an interesting tradition; when the senior class graduated, parents would purchase their children a car as a graduation gift. Now, this might not seem that unusual, as this is kind of a norm. Generally, it is an older used car or a base model Ford, Chevrolet, Honda, Chrysler etc. However, this school was very different. The parents for this graduating class would purchase BMW's, Mercedes, and Porsche, etc. On the graduation day, people in the neighborhood would often go to the school to see all these new expensive high-end cars.

So one day I was chatting with my partner - it was springtime and it was getting close to graduation. I asked her what car her son Adam, who was graduating, had picked out. She gave me this odd look, an annoyed expression and replied: "I would never do that to my son." I was puzzled and asked her what she meant. She responded that she would never take away the opportunity for her son to learn about the hard work it takes to earn something so valuable.

This struck a chord with me and has stuck with me over the years. Being a professional coach and trainer, , this incident has taught me that there are certain lessons in life we do not want to take away from others. To her, this was against her values and integrity as a parent. It would have been no different than stealing a life lesson from her son. And what if that lesson for Adam of working hard, saving for something he really wanted and earning it himself, was the lesson and experience that would have helped define him for the rest of his life?

This is the message I want to strongly convey to you, my fellow coaches. Do not take away opportunities to learn and grow from your clients by giving them advice and suggesting what they should do.

So, when I use the word 'steal', I certainly do not mean removing something physically or taking some kind of intellectual property or a great idea your client has. What I am speaking about is stealing learning opportunities. In our lives, we have opportunities to gain all kinds of things; money, home, cars, and relationships. We also have great opportunities to learn. It is often these opportunities to learn that can have the greatest impact on our lives, resulting in us being able to generate more wealth, relationships, freedom, self-esteem, confidence, and happiness. I would say that it is actually these opportunities to learn about ourselves, that are often the most impactful and powerful lessons in our lives. Resulting in personal breakthroughs and paradigm shifts that allow us to grow as human beings and lead healthier, confident, and more meaningful lives.

At its core, professional coaching is a leadership process. Our mandate, responsibility, and challenge as coaches is to support clients to become the leaders of their lives. This, of course, is not always so easy. Why? Through our growing and maturing process as humans, we start by being dependent on others - Our parents, aunts, uncles, older siblings, teachers, priests, ministers, rabbis are here to teach us the way things are done. They give us advice and tell us what to do. These elders are also instrumental in protecting us from danger and hopefully showing us a path, which leads us to a healthy successful adult life.

During adulthood, we transition through various phases. As adolescents, growing into teenagers we rebel and insist that we (and our peers) are right and the adults are wrong. This is a natural healthy process for us to individualize. This process, which is often a struggle, is an opportunity to define our own set of values and ways to move through the world. Now interestingly enough, you see I mentioned peers. In this process, we often do not cut this invisible cord with parents and teachers so quickly…. but we often replace it with this other group which is usually peers and often society in general.

For many people this process continues into adulthood, with the adult still relying on friends, family, peers, and bosses etc… to tell them what is best for them. They build little internal strength, confidence and only move forward with difficult decisions when other supposedly smarter or more experienced people tell them it is ok or safe to do so. Not through self-reflection and healthy internal dialogue.

Now, I certainly understand that often to make certain decisions we need to explore other points of view, in order to gather more information. However, I can say, from having had thousands of coaching sessions over 18 years, that often my clients, no matter how educated or successful, know very little of themselves and their values. They often make decisions based on other people's thoughts or opinions and beliefs that they have taken on since they were very young. Often not even aware of their own values as adults. At least not until they realize they are unhappy or stuck in a job or relationship that does not support them or bring them happiness.

So, now they are unhappy and stuck with their life. Living a life that others have made for them which is supposed to bring happiness and contentment now brings them despair, confusion, depression and the sense of being stuck. Now, in a real sense, they are. Why? Because they have not learned the skills nor the process of how to explore themselves for what is ultimately meaningful to them.

Now for those that are seekers (like you and me), who are struggling to make sense of this confusion, turn to therapists, clergy, coaches, and mentors. We seek out opportunities to make sense of ourselves and our world.

This is the amazing opportunity we have, as coaches, when these seekers, or as Abraham Maslow puts it, people wanting to self-actualize, become greater than they are by hiring us to work with them. We have the opportunity to work with these clients on an entirely different level. On a level of individualization, of values and of deeper meaning.

So, here is our challenge as professional coaches. Do we continue to be the parental figure that knows the best, and solve problems for our clients or do we accept the challenge to work in a different way? A way that supports clients knowing that they do actually know what is best for themselves. Showing that they have the capability to be true leaders for themselves.

If you thinking that it sounds hard, then you are correct; it is. That is why coaching is so rewarding. Professional coaching requires a solid skill set, practice, constant training, and experience. It also requires us to apply coaching skills to ourselves. I say coaching is a challenging relationship. It will be challenging for our clients, as we will be inviting them to explore some difficult paths. And for us, as we will need to use our skills creatively to facilitate sessions in our clients' best interests.

Now, I understand sometimes clients do not know what they do not know. We can have situations of needing to explain things to clients. However, for most situations especially personal and behavioral problems, coaches that give advice to clients are stealing wonderful learning opportunities from their clients.

If a client comes to us with a typical relationship issue, with a co-worker or boss, and you start giving your opinions, then you are not behaving like a good leadership coach. You are not holding to the principal of your belief that your client is the leader and has many of the answers themselves. You might as well tell your client, "you are so lucky to have hired me because you would have never figured this out yourself. You really needed me and my wisdom to tell you what to do!"

Why do so many coaches struggle to not give advice? Well, we have three main reasons. The first one is that it is what we do in our day to day lives. We have a problem, we fix it? Anyone with any level of success in the world is usually pretty good at solving problems, especially when these problems are not their own (that's another chapter). When our clients talk about their problems, our brains automatically start to solve the problem; it is human nature. Almost like a puzzle that we are challenged to solve. Especially with other problems, we have no internal blocks to solutions as we do not have the faulty beliefs that our clients often do. As one of my mentors used to say, "Coaches need to learn to bite their tongues, and good coaches have very bloody tongues." That is our challenge and our discipline if we want to be great coaches.

Another reason we love to give advice is we enjoy being right. We enjoy solving the problems; it feels good and is a very nice ego stroke! Oh, you have had this problem for how long? Wow! Well, all you have to do is this or that. There you go! Aren't I a genius! Problem solved!

The third reason is that it is just easier. Just tell them the answer. We do not have to work, think hard or challenge our coaching skills. Just tell them your brilliance, get your applause and go on.

However, we do know that it is not always that simple, right?

So, what do I mean? How often do we offer advice, our brilliance and it is not taken, appreciated or acted on? You told them exactly what to do, they may even have thanked you. You're brilliant! Then the next session, no progress except for a grab bag of new excuses! What's wrong with this client? I just told them exactly what to do! They are just not motivated enough! Maybe they need a therapist! However, in reality, what they need is a coach, at least, a good coach.

Human beings look at problems through our own internal filters. We view our world through our maps of experience from growing up and decisions or beliefs created from when we were very young. We often are blind to understanding other solutions presented to us, or repel them like the plague.

One reaction I call the shotgun. No sooner than your sagely advice leaves your lips, your client shoots back. "No, that won't work!" Another variation is "No, I have tried that and everything else, nothing works!" Wow, don't we feel down now as coaches? Gave them our best stuff and they shot it to smithereens!

On top of that look at the game you have set up in your coaching relationship. You give the client advice and if he / she doesn't like it, then you, the coach, better come up with something better! Your client is paying for this remember! He /She hired you because they thought you were smart.

Can you now see how these types of advice-giving coaching sessions puts the pressure on the coach instead of the challenge being on the client? When someone hires a coach, they are not hiring a consultant. Coaches are not hired because of their expertise on particular subjects, or to solve client's problems, but on our ability to offer professional coaching services to support our client, so they can explore their issues and discover possible solutions. If we do not feel that our clients are capable of engaging in a challenging exploration process then we need to question if coaching is the right modality for them.

By offering professional exploratory, challenging coaching sessions, we give our clients the opportunity to understand themselves at a much higher level. We rightfully allow them to take the credit and celebrate their achievements and breakthroughs. We give them time to process and think through what has deep meaning for them and what they want for themselves and others they are responsible for. What significance do family, friends, children, lovers, co-workers and society hold in their beliefs? What do they respect and admire in themselves? It is for the client to discover this and more.

It is worth the challenge my fellow coaches. Join me on the path to becoming a better coach, to become more resourceful and skilled. To be the catalyst of change for our clients.

Steven H. Kiggs

Co-Founder & Director- The Coach Training Academy

Steven is a speaker, author, entrepreneur, coach trainer, and Certified Master Life Coach: a distinction held for coaches who have logged over 5000 hours with clients.

By integrating his extensive life experience and training, he helps people create spectacular change in the quality of their lives. As Steven says, "No one breezes through life. We are all very much the same with just variations of our own issues and demons to work on; that is the human experience".

Facebook – Instagram - LinkedIn - @TheCoachTrainingAcademy

http://www.thecoachtrainingacademy.com/

2

The Real Project Is You

By Ian Hawkins

The most crucial realisation for you to make on your coaching journey is that before you can do all that needs to be done and have everything you desire, you must first focus on who you want to be. Who you are as a human and as a coach is the most important project you will undertake. It's *the* project, and it's one that is never complete. It is also the project that will bring you the most joy and fulfillment because as you become the best possible version of yourself, a world of wonderful opportunities and possibilities will open up for you. It will feel like magic….and well….maybe sometimes it actually is. This project will allow you to attract all that you need as you follow the calling in your heart and soul to help people and positively change the world.

Coaching is a fulfilling experience, but you will face challenges as you journey on. That's a good thing because each challenge will help you to grow as a person and as a coach. It is who you are that will determine how well you navigate each challenge, because the challenges don't disappear as you grow, they actually get bigger. However, if you continue to trust your inner guidance, act on the inspiration and find more internal peace, you will be able to navigate even the biggest challenges with strength and calm.

Contrary to what you have been told, there is no program or business coach that is ever going to give you everything you need to succeed as a coach. Like the rest of your life, there is no magic pill that is going to bring you joy or solve all your problems. Yes, you must do the work, and keep doing the work, because there is no finish line. You will need a tonne of resilience, a healthy dose of determination and 100% commitment to being "all in" on being a coach. Importantly though, it's not about hustling harder, putting in more effort or fighting against the resistance. This will ultimately lead you down the path to burnout and stop you from helping your people - the people you were born to serve. What is required though is incremental steps towards your vision, inspired action, self-compassion and appreciation.

As a coach you must "apply the oxygen mask" to yourself first and that means nurturing your physical, mental, emotional and spiritual health. All 4 areas are crucial to your success and if you neglect one area, it will negatively impact the others. This is a project in self-love, because the more you fall in love with who you are becoming, the more you will be able to do and have. So far you have been on a path to discover the real you, or rather re-discover the real you. The version of you that existed before the people and experiences in your life, took you further and further away from who you are at your core. I want to share with you the most important aspects of your continued rediscovery that will assist you to be the best coach you can be.

Be Decisive

Believe it or not, it is far more important to be decisive and take action than it is to get every decision correct. As you grow as a coach there are lessons you must learn, and the lesson will find you when you are ready. As Jim Rohn stated, *"when the student is ready the teacher will appear"*. If I look back at the early years of my coaching journey, I invested in many programs, each with their promise and each sounded like just what I needed at the time. Every one of them gave me incredible value but also left me feeling disappointed because I was unable to see the financial return on investment that I expected. However, on reflection, every one of those programs gave me exactly the lesson that I needed for my own personal development. What I gained couldn't be measured in currency, but they were invaluable for my growth and coaching. All the money in the world wouldn't be enough for me to give up the difference these programs have had on my life, family and ability to positively impact people's lives. Rest assured though, making decisions will become easier when your find your flow.

Find Your Flow

As a young boy I lived a life of contradiction. I was painfully shy and yet had a deep need for connection. I was a sensitive extrovert trapped in a cocoon of low confidence and emotional confusion. I desperately wanted to be part of the crowd but was often frozen and unable to step out of my comfort zones. Thankfully there was one area that I could feel some semblance of confidence and that was being involved in sport. It proved vital to my growth all through my life. It was also the place that I first experienced "The Zone". That is, being in my natural state of flow. Years later whilst in the early days of my personal development when I learned that flow is possible in everyday life, a light bulb went off in my head and so many pieces of the puzzle fell into place. There are 2 elements of flow that I would like to focus on. The first is your natural gifts and how, by embracing them, you can rapidly accelerate your progress.

You all have the capability to take on most tasks; however, certain areas will allow you to thrive while others will leave you feeling frustrated and exhausted. Get clear on whether you are more detail or people focused, innovative or nurturing, or a combination of any of these. When you find where your preferences lie you will be able to access your personal flow state at will. In flow you feel energised, it seems effortless, time stands still and it's like you know in advance what is going to happen next. It is impossible to feel stress or anxiety when you are in your zone. Flow has taken my coaching to all new levels of impact, helped me to unlock more external confidence and deepened the other element of flow I'll discuss next - my internal connection.

You've all experienced this internal connection; you've felt moments of tingles, a "gut feel, or a gentle knowing in your heart. These experiences of inner guidance are your gateway to The Zone. 10 minutes in the zone will be more beneficial to your coaching than 1 year of forced effort. As a coach this guidance shows up when the right message or question comes into your awareness at just the right time. These messages come from your inner being, the internal guidance system that all humans possess. When you take ego out of the equation and allow your inner being to do the work, it takes all the pressure off. The more you act on this intuition, the more you stop worrying about whether you will "get it right" and instead go into every coaching session, presentation or public speaking event confident in the knowledge that the right message will find you when required. You will continue to unlock more of your flow and as I will discuss later, you will find purpose in your coaching when your gifts and inner guidance merge.

Evolve Your Vision

If you want to be a successful coach, you have to have a compelling, clear and written vision for your future. Not just any vision. One that inspires, comes from your internal guidance system, your inner being and is aligned to your heart and soul. Your Soul Vision. A vision that you have created using only your mental capacity will be full of limitations and will slow your progress. Once you connect within and co-create your Soul Vision, you will be able to connect with only the clients that you were meant to serve and see that there are no limits to the positive impact you can have on this world. Learning to tune into this guidance has changed not only my coaching but my entire life and that of my family. It has helped me to accelerate my growth, create a life full of meaning and most importantly helped me to feel all my favourite emotions every single day. I continue to explore this guidance at a deeper level and evolve my vision on a regular basis. As I have said already, you are never finished.

Heal Yourself

You cannot become the best version of yourself (and the best possible coach) unless you drop the baggage that is holding you back and heal your emotional pain. Think of it this way, from the time you were born, the most important people in your life have unknowingly passed on their behaviour and programming to you. How your mind has processed every experience you have ever had has shaped the person that you have become. While so much of this behaviour has served you well, there are aspects that are holding you and your coaching back. People full of good intentions impacted how you behave from the mistakes that they made when they were younger. These layers of programming and coding have taken you further and further away from your natural self, from who you are at the core of your being. You have already overcome so much on your journey and peeled back many layers of the onion. Emotional, spiritual and energetic healing will accelerate the healing process. Your ability to access your inner guidance will increase to turbo charge your coaching and allow you to keep reconnecting to who you truly are.

Coach With Purpose

"You can't connect the dots looking forward; you can only connect them looking backwards. So you have to trust that the dots will somehow connect in your future. You have to trust in something – your gut, destiny, life, karma, whatever." Steve Jobs

While coaching qualifications are important, your unique background and compelling story is what will attract people into your coaching community. You are an incredibly gifted human, far more credentialled than you give yourself credit for and the more you unlock your gifts, the more you will shine. When you review your life from your earliest memory until the present, you will find common threads in what you repeatedly faced and overcome. The knowledge and skills that you've developed will allow you to guide others to overcome the same challenges. Ask the people you have already helped, and you will see this to be true. You will be both surprised and amazed at the positive impact you have already had on people. This is your gift to the world. When you combine this gift with your flow you will start to coach with purpose.

Rather than being a generalist you will be able to narrow your focus. You become a coach that is true to who you are. Once you connect the dots you will realise that you are still working on improving in these areas. You always will, because it has become your passion. You can stop trying to learn everything about coaching and instead go deep into what you already know. You will be able to take your people on a beautiful, ongoing journey and build a tribe of raving fans who will follow you anywhere. Here you will find your soul aligned purpose and your gift that will help change the world.

You are already sitting on a mountain of value because of who you are. You create incredible value every time you show up as the fullest possible expression of yourself. Take time every day to express full appreciation for all that you are. Breathe, good things take time. Surrender to the process. Trust that everything is working out exactly as it needs to. You are ready to become the coach you were born to be. We're waiting.

Ian Hawkins

Talent Dynamics Consultant, NLP coach, Mindset Mentor, Energetic Healer, Best Selling Author and Speaker

Ian Hawkins is the Founder and Creator of the Personal Alignment Activation Formula™. His mission and passion is to share with the world how to find true meaning in life, experience beautiful emotional states every day and create a lifestyle that excites.

Over the past 15 years Ian has been driven to make the most of his time in this world and decided to devote his life to helping others to do the same. He believes you can Heal your pain, find your Flow, Inspire your world and that your personal evolution is never done, for the growth journey is the best part!

Ian believes that those who desire to make a difference in people's lives shape the world. When they find where they naturally add value to their environment it ripples out and creates an even more awesome world to live in for ALL. When they evolve, transform, & grow into their ultimate self, take inspired action and realise their dreams, goals and desires, it sets a new standard of what's possible and raises the whole universe to a higher level.

Facebook – Instagram - LinkedIn - @ianhawkinscoaching

www.ianhawkinscoaching.com

3

Coaching with Heart and Passion

BY AMY BLOUSTINE

We are in a complex world where, for many, the pursuit of passion and happiness is foremost in their minds. However, sometimes there exists a struggle between pursuing what you love **and** getting paid for it... but should that stop you, and what do you do when you are in this struggle? There is so much talk about the "want to" vs the "have to." How do you navigate this, and what makes the most sense for you?

I can only speak for myself and what I have learned from my life and my coaching experience. What works for me is going to be completely different from what works for you, and that's ok. We don't have to justify what we love and what we want to do. You choose your path, your journey, and what is going to make you happy.

I have people always asking me about my coaching business - how I got into coaching, how I acquire clients, how I built my coaching business, etc. There isn't one answer that fits all, and I am always cautious about how I respond to these questions. How I feel about coaching and how I want to build my business is going to be my version, and everyone has their vision and version, and process for coaching. When I am asked these questions, I turn it around and ask that person why they chose to be a coach, what does coaching mean to them, and what they are looking for in this journey of coaching? No wonder I became a coach, I love to ask the questions.

I remember when I first started coaching, I had a lot of preconceived notions about the type of coaching I "thought" I wanted to do and the type of clients I wanted to work with. Boy! did this change for me very quickly, and everything I thought in the beginning about who I was as a coach and how I was going to do my coaching and grow my business, completely changed, and it changed for the better.

New themes kept emerging with my clients, new approaches, and techniques I was using were evolving, and I completely changed my focus. In the beginning, I think I was so consumed and so worried about the process, that I was not paying enough attention to the experience and the connections. I felt like I had to check off a list during each session.

I think as new coaches, at least for me, we want to make sure that we are doing everything right in the coaching session and doing everything we were taught during our coach training, and I think that's great to build a foundation. For me, in the beginning, it was more transactional than transformational, and what I realized was that, in actual fact, it was both. It's a transactional experience depending on what we are coaching on, but more so, transformational as well. How am I helping the client to maximize their potential, read between the lines, and experience something that they never thought was possible? How am I helping them gain perspective and insight in a completely new way? That seems to be the most transformational part of this for clients. What is the client walking away with from our sessions and the coaching experience?

What I realized, and I think this is essential for my growth as a coach, is that every day I learn something new from my clients. Something that helps me be a better coach and even helps me be a better person. I think that's where the coaching with heart and passion comes from. Every day is new and different, and I am not sure what to expect. What I have learned is each day I am connecting differently; I'm exploring a part of myself that I might not have known was there. I am going deeper with my clients and deeper as a coach. Finding new ways to help my clients achieve a new level within themselves. There is nothing greater than watching a client have that "aha moment," see their face light up when they see something new within themselves, and when a client lands that 'want to' job vs. that 'have to' job; the job they have always wanted and worked so hard to get.

I can easily talk about building a business, all the business basics, but that's not how I have grown or want to grow my business. That's not how I want to coach. I want it to come from a place that means something and has meaning, or else, why would I be doing this? Sure, business fundamentals are essential, but there are plenty of books that teach you how to do this. I read plenty of them when I started coaching, and when I started building my business. Many of them were extremely helpful, and I learned a lot. I also learned a lot from the people I talked to who had been coaching for a long time and even from those who were starting out. My biggest takeaway - listen to your internal voice, don't get caught up in all the noise making.

Stay true to who you are, and what makes sense for you and the work you do - what is most authentic to you. Build the life and the business that is right for you and stop comparing yourself to other coaches and what everyone else is doing. What are your heart and your mind telling you?

Always be eager to learn, listen, and be curious. That has helped me and is helping me as I evolve as a coach. The learning never stops, and the curiosity should always exist inside you. There will always be a new social media platform, a new way to market yourself, or some shiny new object that will "help you build your coaching business and make six figures a year." But where are the emotions, authenticity, transparency, and what matters to you? For me, that's how I can stay connected to my true self; that's how I can grow. I have also learned to understand who I am in this coaching journey and not to limit myself. Commit to something bigger than myself.

I think about those transformational moments with my clients; a look in their eyes, by the way they move or how they are sitting, the language they are using, their words, inflections in their voice, a shift in their energy, the smile in their eyes. That is where I draw my passion from, that is why this comes from the heart. What is it about the questions we ask that gets us to the heart and the passion we have with coaching?

We all know that coaching is about asking powerful questions. We use that as our guide, so ask yourself these questions:

- "Who are you as a coach?"
- "How do you want to connect with your clients?"
- "What is within your power as a coach?"
- "Who is your authentic self as a coach?"
- "How would your clients describe you as a coach?"

I want to bring in the passion and heart piece so you understand where I am coming from and can hopefully identify and connect with it. I know everyone has a different definition of passion and heart, and this will resonate differently for each person. This is how I view this and why it is so vital for me as a coach, but most of all, as a person.

Passion is displayed in a myriad of ways; the tone of voice, body language, or an emotive word. Being passionate is also about the knowledge base you have of a certain subject and never leaving a stone unturned when researching it. Maybe asking the question "what if" instead of saying "only if." Passion shapes who we are, fuels the fire within, and inspires us and opens us up to opportunities and changes around us. That's how I feel about coaching with passion, where the inspiration, motivation, and excitement comes from working with my clients.

The power of passion enables us to show up with confidence; trust ourselves and take risks. It's about having courage; you're living this life by design and not by default. Dare to be the coach you desire with passion and dare to imagine the possibilities. If you feel like this and do this, your clients will feel and do the same. Whatever the passion, there is nothing quite better than being able to experience and live it. Finding your passion is one thing but getting to live your passion is another.

Coaching with a heart will mean something different for me and you, and that's ok. For me, coaching with a heart means authenticity and being present. It is for me something that is so much bigger than me, a work in balance and strength, and going deeper within me and with my clients - that there is something special and compassionate between and among the people in the relationship (those involved in the coaching engagement).

I believe that with my coaching, I am doing something (saying and doing) that is intended to cause a positive and compassionate reaction from the people I am working with. A great quote by Samuel Taylor Coleridge captures the heart piece for me, *"What comes from the heart, goes to the heart."*-

You don't have to do what everyone else is telling you to do and what they are imposing on you. It is all up to you to decide, to discover and to explore. And the best part of this process and exploration is that it will change over time because you will grow as a coach, and most of all, you will grow as a person. I can definitively say that who I was a year into my coaching business, and who I am now five years in, are completely different, and I am so incredibly thankful for that and would not trade it for the world.

As you think about the next steps in your coaching journey, think about creating a new vision of your life while smacked dab in the middle of it, and that's a bold choice, but think about all the possibilities that come with it. Exercise your capacity to dream and set an intention to coach with passion and heart. Think about what the whole story of your life will be - are you doing what you want?

Amy Bloustine

Certified Life and Career Coach, Time Management
Coach and Trained Recovery Coach

Amy's goal is to help clients identify and overcome obstacles that are preventing them from being the best version of themselves-whatever that means for them. Whether they're looking for solutions to specific personal or professional challenges they are facing or if feeling stuck.

One of Amy's coaching strengths is to visualize the overall picture of complex problems, and then strategically deconstruct them to identify solutions with her clients. Every client is unique. Their goals, obstacles, passions; they're all personal and highly individual.

Amy's coaching philosophy evolves and grows with each client. Her coaching style is creative, thought-provoking, and collaborative. She works with her clients as a collaboration, and she creates a safe, trusting, comfortable environment in which she and her clients can learn and grow. The ultimate goal with her coaching is to help her clients discover how to figure things out for themselves, solve problems independently, find their way, and let them discover the solution that already exists within.

www.amybloustinecoaching.com

Facebook – Linkedin amybloustinecoaching

4

ENGAGE Your Brave Life

BY MEL LEOW

You come home after a full day's work to find that the electricity has been turned off.

You check your main distributor board to see if it was a trip from a singular switch, or the entire home. If it was the latter, you frantically run to the kitchen to observe the contents of your fridge to gauge how long the power has been off.

If you are like me, you would take the initiative to go over to your neighbors to get an update on the power outage. You would then call up your local electricity company to find out when the power would be reconnected. And if the outage persists, you plan your possible contingencies - where you would eat, shower and sleep.

In life it is similar and yet ironically, we may *not be aware* that the power has been turned off. At times we may be numbed to the fact that we have been living *without power* for many years now. What do I mean by that?

You see, we all have a Vision, Purpose, Plan, Dream, Goal or important Life Focuses that we would like to pursue, attain, achieve, realize, reach and fulfill. But along the journey towards these milestones and anticipated achievements, we get sidelined, distracted, preoccupied and allow feelings of apprehension, hesitation, insecurity and even fear to creep in. And subsequently, the busyness and apathy of life locks us into a vicious default cycle that takes us far away from what we really want and desire in life.

Are you connected or disconnected from the power source today?

In my corporate experience, I have worked with hundreds of leaders, talents and entrepreneurs from the Asia Pacific region and even though they are such amazing individuals in their own right, I have found *3 distinctive traits* that set the extraordinary ones apart from the rest.

The *first* is the elevated *"Intrinsic Drive"* that catapults them to stand out in their roles and industry. Their 'initiative' attitude coupled with their innovative mindset often accompanies their high-octane contagious energy and engagement. It is the *fire in their eyes* and *their captivating presence,* that you instantly feel by being around them for just a while.

The *second* is the extreme discipline of *"Being Focused".* According to Malcolm Gladwell in his book "Outliers" he states that 10,000 hours of "deliberate practice" is needed to become world-class in any field. In part there is truth in it, and yet the more important challenge is asking, *"What is the outcome of the 10,000 hours practice without Focus?".* Being focused is not about doing the most work, it is about doing the most important work with the highest quality and output productively.

The *third* is their motivation to *"Achieve and Succeed (Much) More"* within a given time. And it seems as though they have the unfair advantage of extra hours in a day, to achieve the astonishing results. It is not perfection they are seeking; it is progress. They know things they get involved in will never get perfected, but they do not stop trying. *Mark Victor Hansen says it best, "Don't wait until everything is just right. There will always be challenges, obstacles and less than perfect conditions... get started now. With each step you take, you will grow stronger and stronger, more and more skilled, more and more self-confident and more and more successful."*

It is often easier to come up with excuses to avoid starting something like the infamous, *"If only I had more experience, more guts, more brains, more support, more time, more money, more resources"* than to actually begin. You may be a person who is:

- *Desperately wanting to quit smoking, or*
- *Resolved to move into a new relationship and start fresh, or*
- *Determined to start an exercise regime or diet, or*
- *Bored of their high-paying job and want to become an entrepreneur or*
- *Wanting to kick their fear of heights, cats, or your mother in law.*

Making any one of these decisions above and then taking action with a solid effort requires *resilience*, a level of *willingness to risk* and a whole lot of *spirit*.

In life, you can choose to stay in default mode and continue living in that state of experience and acceptance, based on your years of conditioning. Or, you can choose to break free from the walls of your self-limiting beliefs, your comfort zone and even your fears and start living the life you truly desire.

The question is *"Are you brave enough?"*

Every example I shared above, from the ex-smoker, the new relationship, the exercise-diet-junkie, the entrepreneur and the fear conqueror - are *real people* I have encountered through my journey as a Coach. Each of them is now living the life they want, on their own terms.

One common thread I have noticed is they each have identified a *Brave-outcome: a bigger, brighter goal which acts as a positive and powerful reinforcement for what they ultimately want.* This is often tied to a deeper, more grandeur meaning that impacts their lives, versus merely focusing on the push factor to solve the problem of an unwanted behaviour.

Through all the years I've been coaching, I've discovered that there are *4 E's to a Brave Outcome,* to motivate and inspire a person to stick to what they set out to undertake in their life.

The First of the E's is ENERGY.

Every living organism on our planet has an energy signature. Science has proven that all matter produces energy and can cause a reaction or result. Even the words we choose to speak, every thought and belief we carry, produces an energy and it can direct or run our life.

"Have you ever been sucked into somebody's chaotic life drama?" It can get very disempowering and negative, as you watch a once-loving couple tear each other apart. Conversely, *"Have you ever been surrounded by people who are high on life, with their full-on positive attitude and they go out and change the world?"* This scenario can be extremely rewarding and inspiring. You see, *energy is contagious.* Whether it's good or bad, positive or negative; energy can impact, affect and influence everyone around it.

Being aware of the energy you produce when faced with life scenarios and big decisions about your dreams and goals can help you decide where you need to be. The right energy can make you feel excited, happy, motivated, relaxed, and even rested. It's a good indicator you're ready to step ahead.

Energy is also what separates people who have recognized their drive from those who are still looking for it. More energy is found from people who are living their life *"on purpose"* as they project confidence from the inside out. You can intuitively tell if they are seamlessly moving in alignment with the frequency of their intended actions, without reluctance or struggle.

What Energy Frequency is required for you to go to where you want to go?

The second E is EXPECTATIONS.

Having expectations is normal. Expectations are necessary and is a healthy way of setting the right path and direction. Expectations are especially effective when they are communicated with clarity and heart. They set people up for success instead of failure.

When I work with highly talented young people in an organization, an area of disappointment is when their leaders fail to provide them with a clear direction. To make matters worse, these leaders often employ a micro-managing, non-trusting, authoritarian style across the board with everyone.

Stating expectations creates greater clarity and draws a line in the sand between autonomy, assurance and accountability. When you set right expectations, you begin to consider alternative ways to make things better. Expectations remove the need for chance and, they help set out a **R.O.A.D**-map toward Success.

R is for Rationale. *Why am I doing what I am doing?* If this does not connect back to the bigger reason, a vision or calling for your life, then whatever you begin may not withstand the test of time.

O is for Outcome. *What's the result you're looking for?* This represents a tangible standard or benchmark which is essential to meet or exceed. For example:

- *What does good look like?* and
- *What does great look like?*

A is for Actions. *What specific actions are you willing to take?* These are the critical tasks that need to be taken with the right steps in place.

D is for Deadline. *When does it need to be completed?* Expectations that aren't time-bound are simply wishes on a prayer. It might not happen.

What Expectations have you set-in-line with what you want to achieve?

<u>The third E is EXPLORATIONS.</u>

I love travelling to new lands and being exposed to eclectic cultures. By simply crossing over a geographic border into another country, you can experience the distinctions. For example, the difference between the USA and Canada, France and Belgium, Nigeria and Ghana, Australia and New Zealand, Thailand and Malaysia, and more.

As a result of the Explorations of people; new frontiers can be embraced which go beyond community and ethnic borders. Exploration is one of the reasons we now have *new innovations* in every socio-economic segment on the planet. Here are just a few examples of innovation as a result of exploration: *Airbnb for accommodations, Amazon for online shopping, Facebook for creating community, Uber for transport, Waze for providing road directions, WeChat for payment gateway, Zoom for webinar conferencing* and the list goes on.

I was exposed to Social Entrepreneurship in 2011. As an explorer, that exposure led me to initiate a project to support *Founders of Social Enterprises* in Nigeria. We offered equipping and coaching programs, to help new leaders through an often-lonely journey as *Change Agents* in their communities.

In the beginning many close friends were shocked I would choose to extend my coaching work to Africa, let alone Nigeria. They would state with concern, *"Be careful, Nigerians are like this… and like that…"*

My persistent reply was, *"There are many good and bad people anywhere around the globe."* If I had listened and followed what my circle of friends had said, I would've never explored into Nigeria over the past few years. From a tiny project, **Catalyst** has become a growing movement with a BIG Vision to ignite 10,000,000 lives across Africa over the next decade.

"Until you cross the bridge of your insecurities, you can't begin to explore your possibilities." – **Tim Fargo**

Explorations allow us to break open our boundaries of assumptions, perceptions, indifference and even our misconceptions. Explorations also confirm our current reality isn't necessarily a true map of our destiny. Explorations enlarge our ability to dream and challenge our belief system, making things that once were unimaginable, achievable.

Unbroken by blindness in 1998, international motivational speaker Mark Pollock, went on to compete in ultra-endurance races across deserts, mountains, and the polar ice caps. Pollock was the first blind person to ever race to the South Pole. He's also a two-time Commonwealth Games medalist for rowing and is an icon for resilience and achieving more than thought possible.

In 2010, Mark was left paralyzed after falling from a second story window. He is now exploring the intersection where humanity and technology collide. He is catalyzing collaborations that have never been attempted before. Recently, Mark launched an Exoskeleton Access Programme at Dublin City University to provide universal access to Ekso Bionics robotic legs for the paralyzed, stroke patients and other neurological conditions for a nominal fee. Through the Mark Pollock Trust, he is unlocking $1 billion dollars in funding to cure paralysis in our lifetime.

What Explorations are you embarking on that will challenge you to move forward?

The fourth E is EXPERIENCES

When my wife and I discovered our youngest son was dyslexic, we were a little distraught. We didn't realize he had suffered in silence until we recalled the many occasions where he came home from school unable to grasp the simplest of spelling, writing and math assignments. We were told by experts his brain was *wired differently.*

I initially blamed myself for not realizing his condition earlier and took it upon myself to find ways to help him. I even found a program in Auckland, New Zealand where a trainer had designed a proven methodology to help dyslexic people read better. Upon completing the program, I rushed back eager and excited to test my new-found knowledge.

Eventually, with a great deal of discipline, our son slowly but surely started recognizing words as he read. His vocabulary grew day by day. What we failed to realize was the methodology he learned, like everything else in life, required consistent action for maximum results.

Nothing can be built without a foundation of accumulated and purposeful action over time. In any *Brave-outcome*, there must be a compound effect of decisiveness and commitment to craft and an appreciation of our intended result.

Experiences become the bedrock of learning. They can be the teacher of all things. Our experience with our son taught us a hard lesson, *"Giving up at the halfway point only resets the envisioned nature of the experience. This halfway effort gives way to lethargy about ever reaching the desired outcome."*

Experiences give birth to *Milestones,* crafted and forged through the fiery trials of life. Each milestone reached can become a stepping stone to the next level. Don't despise days of small beginnings or give up. Instead press on. Every little action you take on a daily basis can change the course of your life. *Every milestone counts.*

There is a silver lining to the story of our son. Today, he has developed a fondness for writing on his iPad with its attached keyboard. This has given us a fresh start and enthusiasm about his overall learning experience. In fact, I am proud to say he is progressing amazingly well and has improved his ability to communicate confidently.

Experiences are also a mirror of the stories we tell ourselves. These stories are often filled with half-truths about what's possible and what's impossible. We often get stuck because we can only choose to believe in one part of the truth and not the other. It is like the constant narrative some people tell themselves saying they aren't good enough or they won't amount to anything.

One narrative I had was that I could never get past my fear of heights. Once I learned I could kick it, I challenged my fear at every opportunity. I started pushing myself to face my fears, trying anything scary from bungie jumping to sky-diving, to canyoning and to riding the rollercoasters at every theme park I visited.

I like what Steve Pavlina shared *"Don't die without embracing the daring adventure your life was meant to be."* It is so true for my life - when I embraced the adventures of the next height challenge, it became a new part of me that I began to accept and appreciate. When I changed my narrative, I changed my experiences. The same can happen to you.

What new Experiences are you engaging in, to change your life forever?

As you reflect on the 4 E's to a Brave-outcome, allow yourself to be realigned and refocused to a new vision toward your desired destination. However challenging it may be, when you commit to it habitually, you will change the course of your life forever. Don't spend another moment living in default or for someone else. Instead, live in a way that brings you closer to your purpose and your power source.

Your time is now. Will you say yes to your Brave New Life?

Mel Leow

Executive Leadership & Life Coach, Catalyst & Mentor Coach
Founder of APIC and Catalyst

Over the past 15 years, I have been privileged to coach, train and impact thousands of leaders and talents from top organizations across the Asia Pacific region.

It has always been my desire to learn and glean from the best. I am humbled to have been trained/mentored by John C. Maxwell and Team, Sir John Whitmore (GROW Model), Dr. Richard Bandler (NLP Co-Creator) and have worked with other experts in their field like Natalie Ashdown, Patrick Merlevede, W Mitchell and the late Marilyn Powell.

Mel is the co-author of "Bring Out Their BEST" – Inspiring a Coaching Culture at the Workplace, that features 40 Best Practice stories from organizations across the Asia Pacific Region. www.apicoaching.com/best

Mel's new book coming out in March 2020 is entitled "ENGAGE – How to Stop Living in Default and Start Living the Life You Desire".

E: mel@apicoaching.com

W: www.apicoaching.com (APIC)

W: www.iamcatalyst.live (Catalyst)

L: www.linkedin.com/in/coachmel

5

Reinventing Myself

BY JAYITA ROY

An enriching roller-coaster journey from being a small-town girl to a successful HR professional to a coach

"What do you want to be when you grow up?" Like many of you, while growing up, I was constantly asked this question and over time my answers changed from a designer to a doctor to a pilot. But one desire that remained constant was that, beyond my education, I wanted to be an independent person. However, like many others, my life was pre-decided by elders at home.

Coming from a small town in India, avenues were limited. It didn't take long for me to understand that I need to experience the world beyond my hometown to achieve my dream. However, no one around me resonated with my thoughts. This 'desire' to be independent was beginning to seem unattainable . No one, especially no girl in the family and friends circle stepped out of the house at an early age. This made it even more difficult to sell my idea of stepping outside the protected shelter of my parents. Discouragement poured in from all corners . I didn't really know how to materialize my dream. Only way was to influence my parents and convince them to support my decision. The consistent visible confidence in myself instilled confidence in my parents to approve my decision. This was the beginning of my transformation journey and a step towards realising my dream. After school, I walked into an unknown big city, 2000 miles away from my home, with dreams of building my own identity and to be an independent person. I am grateful to my parents, especially my mother, for making it possible for me. This would never have been possible without her.

Things changed a lot when I moved from a small town to a big city, especially since I was alone. Everything that I saw, felt and heard were different in all dimensions. Since then life has been an enriching roller coaster ride. I still remember how I even struggled to speak English as at home I used to communicate in the local language. I was bullied for my English communication skills. Quite often, my capabilities were judged by my ability to speak fluent English. There were days I felt sad, but I never allowed it to discourage myself. I put my mind to overcome this challenge and it did.

Now, when I look back, those days built the foundation of who I am today. Of course, there were moments of self-doubt and despair. But," believing in myself" helped me to break the stereotypes and gave me the confidence to bounce back every time I experienced a downward spiral. The decision to move out of my home and to lead a responsible independent life was one of the early turning points in my life. I learnt how important it was to trust intuition when in a dilemma, to treat mistakes as building blocks for learning and most importantly, to believe in yourself.

Early learning in life - Believe in yourself and the world will believe in you too

Introduction to Coaching

I chose my career in Human Resources (HR) in the corporate world. I rose the corporate ladder quickly and held various senior leadership roles at a young age. As my career progressed, quite often I found people approaching me to discuss their aspirations, career growth and challenges. It used to come naturally to me to have conversations that helped them get different perspectives and directions. I started receiving positive feedback. These positive feedbacks were extremely encouraging. It developed an interest in me to find out more about coaching conversations. This was when I enrolled in a formal coaching training program in 2008. Since then coaching in some way or the other has been part of my life. However, I never planned to be a coach; I was happy climbing up the corporate ladder, until I experienced coaching myself.

Coaching Reinvented My Being

As life progressed, I found myself stuck in an unhappy marriage that led to divorce. In my society, even today, divorce is a stigma. I was surrounded with diverse views and judgmental comments. I hit an all-time low score in my confidence. I immersed myself into work, popped anti-depressant pills, did everything that my doctor and counsellor asked me to. But nothing had a lasting impact. I was in a zone in which I was ready to do anything and everything to get back to myself, to be happy again, but I didn't really know "HOW". I started doubting myself in almost all aspects of life. One sleepless night, I got this life changing idea of engaging a life coach. Next moment I knew I was browsing through Google to find one.

I made one of the best decisions I could have ever made for myself - I invested in coaching. With my life coach, I started to move from being stuck to unstuck in life. Interesting part of coaching was that I realised the external factors around me did not change at all. It was the same people around me, the same situation, but what changed was my perspective, my ability to deal with the same situation differently and in a much effective way. I was happy again. Working with my coach gave me much more than what I had signed for. My coach not only helped me to get unstuck but also helped me to rediscover my passion for coaching.

Joy of Rediscovering the 'Coach' Within Me

My coaching experience was so profound that it touched me deeply. The coaching journey transformed my life. I developed a strong feeling to amplify this magical experience to many more. It got me thinking of how fulfilling the experience would be to pursue a career which positively impacted people's lives. I had a strong feeling that this was my calling in life. I had a "Eureka moment!". There's no better feeling in the world than experiencing the "A-HA!" moment of discovering the purpose of one's life.

To further enhance my coaching skills, I enrolled in a coaching course and graduated as an ICF Coach while continuing with my corporate job.

Initial Roadblock

Although I had been coaching people, I realised I needed to put my complete focus in coaching to build my coaching brand. Being in a full-time job, didn't make this seem feasible.

'Do I leave my job?' was the next question I was thinking. But the thought of leaving a source of sustainable income wasn't appealing. I couldn't find anyone to seek advice. No one in my family or friends had an experience of setting up something of their own. Most of the people I knew didn't even know what coaching was. They thought I was crazy to leave a highly paid secure job. I started getting tons of advice on why I should stick to my job. I was told several stories of how people failed when they 'chased' similar aspirations. It created ripples of fear within me. But thankfully, I didn't allow these discouragements to dismiss my dream; instead, I decided to seek help. I started scouting for people with similar experiences. I decided to invest in a coach once again. I contacted my coaching teacher and I am grateful that she agreed to coach me and partner with me in my journey.

We built a plan. She guided me to take SMART action and gave perspectives that helped me to broaden my thoughts. Yet another time, working with my coach revolutionised my life. Not only did she help me make progress with my coaching roadmap, she helped me discover my talent for writing and helped me eliminate my self-limiting doubts.

However, the advice of sticking to my job continued to flow from all directions. I realised I needed to build an emotional shield around me so that I don't get perturbed by discouraging comments or advices. But even after that, a crippling sense of fear kept surfacing from time to time.

Overcoming Fears

Overcoming fear has been the biggest challenge and greatest milestone in my journey thus far. Every time someone said something negative, it raised several doubts. Often, I felt paralysed by my fear. However, there was a part of me that didn't want to give up. I knew it was important for me to arrest my fears. I did an exercise of writing down all my fears and emotions associated to the fears - I called it as "my fear list". With this exercise, I gained clarity about my two biggest fears:

- Fear No. 1: I pay my own bills so will I continue to have the certainty of financial stability?

- Fear No. 2: Starting on my own at this stage of my career, am I risking my professional growth?

Nailing down my biggest fears helped me to move forward. Instead of allowing my fears to clip my dream, I built antidotes to my fears.

- Antidote 1: Planning -

I made a financial plan and took significant action to have the funds that will give me certainty of finances.

- Antidote 2: Defining Growth –

When I delved a little deeper, I realised that this journey of mine was extremely enriching. It was all about investing in myself emotionally, acquiring knowledge, building skills, which was allowing me to become the best version of myself and that enabled me to best serve people. This is certainly adding to both my professional and personal growth trajectory.

I learnt that focusing on achievement is much more empowering than thinking about failure.

The Driving Forces

Yes! Finding my purpose in life has been extremely gratifying. However, I used to often wonder why fulfilling my dream of becoming a coach was so important to me? Afterall I had already built a career for myself. Was this transition necessary at this life stage? What was driving me to put so much effort into overcoming my fear? What was driving me to leave the comfort of my job and dive into a new world?

It didn't take long for me to unveil the driving forces within me

- If I don't work for my own dream, who else will?
- Fear of regret - If I don't act now, I may regret in future for not taking enough action to materialise my dream.
- And most importantly, never have I felt this sense of fulfilment when my clients discover the "aha" moment, in any other vocation. The experience of witnessing the spark in their voice and the twinkle in their eyes when they unlock an issue or cast a whole new light on a situation is priceless.

Here I am, conquering the fear of bidding adieu to a successful corporate life, leaving behind the handsome monthly pay checks and the comfort of a secured job, to pursue my dream of transforming people's lives through coaching.

"Believing in myself" helped me to break the stereotypes and overcome personal and professional barriers. There is no doubt that every one of us is going through a personal journey. No two people's journeys are the same. Your journey is unique to you. However, how you approach your life journey will make it either ordinary or extraordinary.

If you dare to dream, if you are thinking to make a life changing decision, or if you want to keep moving purposefully, it's time to take concrete actions. Don't settle for less. I am sharing my top techniques that have worked well for me.

1. Self-Belief

What would you dare to achieve if you believed in yourself with an unparalleled attitude that you had no fears of rejection or failure whatsoever? Isn't this thought so empowering? "Believe in yourself" is one of the wise old sayings that works like a miracle. Of course, there will be moments of self-doubt. Our confidence can wax and wane all through our lives. It is raised when we receive appreciation, overcome barriers or experience a win. At the same time, it takes a backseat when we are criticized, rejected, or experience a lack of external recognition. I, therefore suggest not to become overly dependent on external validation to boost your self-worth or to endorse yourself, instead take specific actions needed to nurture it. Without our permission, no one can make us feel inferior.

"What the mind can conceive and believe, it can achieve."- Napoleon Hill

2. Listening to Your Intuition.

Are you unsure about your decision to follow your dreams? Are you in a dilemma? If you find yourself nodding to these questions, try listening to your intuition. Trusting your intuition boosts your self-confidence. If you have not used your intuition before, carefully observe your intuition and test it. Intuition is an ability we all have; one we can develop into a skill.

Intuition is an important but unrecognized part of our lives. It is that integral part of us that always knows the correct answer. Intuition is information from our highest level of consciousness. Most of us constantly receive its messages but choose to ignore them. Our rational mind gives us the logical reasons to ignore the intuitive impulse. When we ignore our intuitive mind, it speaks to us less often. Intuition is built like a muscle. The more it is used the stronger it grows.

"I believe in intuitions and inspirations. I sometimes FEEL that I am right. I do not

KNOW that I am."— Albert Einstein

3. Power of Fear

Fear, if utilised well, can be the biggest source of power. Embrace your fear, because if you don't feel any, you're probably not pushing yourself hard enough. Approach your fear like a new project. Note down all your fears and its associated feelings that's stopping you from following your dreams. Mostly all fears arise from one or two bigger underlying reasons. Once you identify the reasons, you will find yourself in a much better position to build a plan to deal with it. When you plan, you'll often discover some hard truths about what it will take to accomplish your dreams. This can feel a bit uncomfortable because you're no longer in a happy imaginary world. But discovering these facts as early as possible gives you the ability to quickly validate and adjust your plan. This maximizes your effectiveness and lifts your confidence. Therefore, I encourage you to embrace your fear and make it your weapon to raise yourself.

"Fear doesn't exist anywhere except in the mind". - Dale Carnegie

4. Investing in yourself

When was the last time you invested in yourself? There is no more profitable investment than investing in yourself. Whether it's investing in learning a new skill, expanding your knowledge, or tapping into your creative side, developing yourself personally or professionally is integral. This is one of the most powerful tools that makes you who you are and builds the foundation of your future. Where you will stand and what new things you will be capable of doing tomorrow will largely depend on what you do to improve yourself today. Without improving yourself consistently, it would be impractical to picture a different outcome or even future from the one you have right now, as you will be no different tomorrow from the person you are today. Prioritize yourself and take the time to invest. As the adage goes:

"Make yourself a priority. At the end of the day, you are your longest commitment"

5. Learn, Unlearn and Relearn

It is essential to have an open mindset to learn and unlearn along the journey. As Tony Robbins says – you clearly decide what it is that you are absolutely committed to achieving; you are willing to take massive action; you notice what's working or not, and you continue to change your approach until you achieve what you want.

"Most of the important things in the world have been accomplished by people who have kept on trying when there seemed no hope at all"- Dale Carnegie

6. Finding an Ally

An ally can be your mentor or your coach who can guide you through to achieve your goal, offer emotional support and give you right feedback to ensure you are on the right track. So, one of the most important things you can do is finding a right ally for yourself, someone you aspire to be like and with whom you can confidently discuss situations as they arise. An ally can be a golden ticket to success.

"Surround yourself only with people who are going to take you higher."— *Oprah Winfrey*

And to all aspiring coaches, if you are out there to be a coach, experience the journey of coaching yourself first. Until you know the taste of it you can never pin down the various unsaid flavours of coaching. Being a coach and being coached, I can confidently say coaching is the only platform wherein one receives more than what one has signed for. I am a living testimony of this.

As Michelle Obama said, *"Your story is what you have, what you will always have. It is something to own."* So, what are you waiting for? Your dream isn't going to actualise itself! Take responsibility and create your life. Infuse your life with real actions. Don't wait for it to happen.

Build the conviction and confidence to pursue your dreams. Take control of your self-limiting beliefs and boost your self-belief by investing in yourself. Investment in yourself will consistently raise your bar and will take you places. Take your self-belief to the peak where nothing can hold you back. Feel proud, empowered and keep striving to be the best version of yourself.

Empower yourself by investing in yourself.

Jayita Roy

Certified Career & Life Coach, International Human Resources Professional.

Jayita has a master's in business administration, and quickly rose through the ranks where she has forged a formidable career for over 15 years in HR Leadership over different fast-paced industries.

Self-confidence, focus, agility, high results-orientation and a strong personal drive have been inherent qualities that Jayita has demonstrated in all aspects of her life.

Different life changing experiences and her passion for developing people kindled her interest and zeal for helping others to achieve their goals on both personal and professional fronts. With her abilities to connect with individual of all ages, ethnicities, beliefs and adapt to different cultures and geographies, Jayita's ethos as a Coach is to encourage her clients to reflect on their whole selves both in work and life. Life in all its forms can be overwhelming and Jayita strives to encourage her clients to restructure, simplify, validate and define their objectives through to realization.

Jayita's areas of expertise as a Coach are in Leadership and Executive Development, Career Transitions and Career Management, Personal Effectiveness and Fulfilment. Jayita is also passionate about working specifically with women in areas such as self-care, divorce and empowerment.

Website: www.readysteadyshift.com
Email Id: jayita@readysteadyshift.com
LinkedIn – https://www.linkedin.com/in/jayita-roy-4562a311/
Facebook - royjayita3105
Instagram – jayi.roy

6

Stripping away the Hype Jargon and Mystery

BY DAVID TAYLOR

Roy Mcavoy

"This is everything, ain't it, this is the choice it comes down to, this is our immortality"

His Caddy

"You don't need to be thinking immortality, you need to think hit the seven iron"

From the film, Tin Cup

Picture the scene – you have been invited to Abu Dhabi to give a Keynote to 600 plus people on 'Emotional Intelligence'. Prior to the session you speak with the organisers, some nominated attendees and even the main sponsor, and as a result of those discussions you have a dawning observation:

Everyone has a different definition of 'Emotional Intelligence'. Of course, you always knew this was going to be the case, however it is reasonable to think that across all the meanings, there would at least be some consistency. And indeed, there is - some people did actually use the words 'emotion' and/or 'intelligence' – many others didn't!

That is the exact position I was in. I mentioned this to my Psychology Advisor, Clair Carpenter, a Harvard Psychologist. Her reply will stay with me forever:

"Oh, come on David – how many people do you need in a room, to have a disagreement?"

"Two?" I replied, tentatively

"No, David – One" she replied with some glee, before adding:

"The first sign of madness is talking to yourself; the second sign is arguing with yourself, and the final sign is losing the arguments!"

Of course, Clair is right – about both her answer and its wider implication, which is:

No word has any meaning other than the meaning you choose to give it – and before you yell Dr. Johnson at me, I whisper the same name back. After all, it was he who compiled the very first dictionary, and in doing so he literally made up the meaning of each and every word – well, at least every word around at the time.

Just as with 'emotional intelligence' we all face the same challenge with 'Transformation'; 'Change; and even 'communication' – oh! the irony.

And 'Coaching'

Here are 3 definitions for you – please choose which you will adopt, believe and apply:

1. Assuming you are reading this final chapter last, you will have read a lot of different definitions of what coaching is – so believe whichever one you want.

2. Make up your own – people often do, so why not you? My most recent favourite was "Coaching is not Mentoring". Good luck with that one!

3. Go with mine – compiled for my book 'The Naked Coach'. Coaching is:

Any and every intervention that enables people, teams and organisations to be their very best

Made your choice?

OK – here are the 7 Key Actions to take to be a successful coach, in this wonderful, exciting and fast-moving business age, and world:

It's Not About You

It's never about you. Just as teaching is not about the teacher and leadership is not about the leader, coaching is not about the coach – it is all about the person you are coaching – your Coachee. So, tell stories that are relevant to them, not you; share practical examples that are relevant to them, not you; and use clear, concise and compelling language that they will understand. The brain doesn't just switch off from what it cannot understand, it is actively pushed against it.

A great opening question to understand the person sitting opposite you is:

'How's it going?'

And then listen, really listen

Does this person use long or short sentences (copy), voice inflections (copy) and eye contact (copy) – without, of course, them realising that is what you are doing!

The Formula for Guaranteed Success

For 'The Naked Leader' book I wanted to take every model for success, leadership and coaching, and simplify it down to something that would fit on a business card. It took over a year, and after much academic, leadership and psychological input, and a further year of piloting with many organisations, we came up with what we humbly call 'The Formula for Guaranteed Success' (FGS).

Naked Leader Formula for Guaranteed Success

This Science of Success is what we do as individuals, teams and organisations whenever we achieve success, as defined by us. It's what happens: the FGS is a summary of every 'success' model with no hype, jargon or mystery. It's simple, not simplistic – and therein lies its practical power.

Use it – it works, as proved by organisations, leaders and people the world over – ranging from Veolia to The Princes Trust, from Chinese Universities to Ford and to the NHS too.

Know Where You Want To Go – Outcomes

There are so many names for it – 'Aim', 'Goal', 'Vision', 'Purpose' etc. etc. The over-riding key question for your coachee is this:

"What's your Outcome?"

Possibly the most powerful question, because:

It gives all the power to the other person, and away from you;

It is totally non judgemental;

It can be applied everywhere and with anyone. In one to one Coaching, in teams, projects, meetings etc. etc. etc.

And when it comes to Outcomes:

Guide your coachees to focus on what they want, not what they don't – as our thoughts will move to whichever we choose.

Separate the 'what' from the 'how' – keep people focused on 'what'. This is tough. Because our brain's primary function is survival, it will want to either rush to the 'how' or wallow in the 'now'. Keep moving them back to the outcome.

Set a standard for themselves that is higher than anyone else can ever reasonably expect of them – this gives the perfect balance between going for the impossible – never motivating for anyone - and choosing an outcome they can achieve with their eyes closed.

And in a business coaching session it is helpful to have a defined financial value attached to the outcome.

Know Where You Are Now - Reality

What is their present position? When they assess this, ask questions that help your coachee to see it as it is – no better, no worse. One way to achieve this is to remove any judgements or opinions in the language that they use, and simply state facts.

Identify what strengths, passions and ideas they have that would help move them closer to their outcome. Unleashing the potential in people is an absolute given for organisations worldwide going forward. Also, ask them for anything they need to do differently, to achieve their outcome.

Next, plant the grain of pain in their minds, so they really will do something as a result of your coaching session. Do this by asking them what would happen going forward if nothing changed at all – what outcome would be achieved then?

Know What You Have To Do To Get To Where You Want To Go - Choices

Everyone goes on about Change, which, to cut a very long word and idea very short, never works – never has, never does and never will. It is insulting (we hate being told to change), irrelevant (we are changing all the time), meaningless (because different people will want to change different things) and finally very boring (wouldn't you rather have deep root canal surgery at your dentist, without anaesthetic, than read another manual on Total Quality Management?) Focus instead on choice.

"Imagine if you simply could not fail – what would you do?" – What choices would you have? People always have more choices than they first believe they have.

Finish this part by 'bigging' them up – in a very focused, factual, scientific way – by quoting the chances against them being born – it's one in ten trillion to the power of four, according to Richard Dawkins – professor of Science at Oxford University, England. And some think it's even more unlikely than that. https://bit.ly/38V2c4t

Do It! – Action and Persistence and #nevergiveup

Do something - whether it is a choice your coachee has made, or one you have suggested, or whatever – DO IT! There is only one way to know whether something will 'work' or not, and that is to do it and see!

Don't wait for others or expect others to do as you do – take ownership of yourself.

So, DO SOMETHING! If it takes you closer to your outcome, do more of the same and keep going until someone tells you to stop - seek forgiveness not permission. If it takes you further away, then do something else, and if that doesn't "work" then do something else etc.

Just as you learned to walk.

Have fun!

People are more open minded when they are laughing and happy. Although this is the shortest point of the 7 it is in many ways the most important. Use how-to's and stories from movies and TV and books and plays.

Now, please, Go Coach, Go Help others, Go Be You…

You will be guiding people to places that they didn't know existed . . .

They will be excited, scared, motivated, challenged, curious and anxious.

All at once.

I know you will serve them well.

David X

David Taylor

Founder of Naked Leader, Author

David is a recognized global authority on leadership. He unleashes the unlimited potential within us all, enabling people, teams and organisations to achieve levels of success they never thought possible. His Clients range from Chief Executives to world leaders and from athletes to those in greatest need.

He is the Founder of Naked Leader, author of the fastest selling business book in the world: The Naked Leader, and four global follow-ups.

David has featured in 3 TV Series and keynoted in 74 countries - over a million people have attended a David Taylor event.

He is The Business Ambassador for The Prince's Trust, Honorary Professor of Leadership at Ulster University Business school and Chair of Naked Leader China – helping Western companies succeed in China, and vice versa.

www.nakedleader.com

Facebook – Instagram – LinkedIn - @nakedleader

7

You've Got What It Takes

BY SNEHAL R. SINGH

"I do not try to dance better than anyone else. I only try to dance better than myself."

~ Mikhail Baryshnikov

Jan 11, 2011, was the day I still remember vividly. It was my last day of the job with a multinational company and a great paycheck every month. However, I was looking for something else. I was looking for freedom. I wanted to change the lives of many and inspire many and was not ready to follow the rules set by traditional companies. I was very confident, even then, that the only way to do this was through Training and Coaching.

The first thing I did was get myself certified as a Dale Carnegie trainer, and instantly updated my profile everywhere. All set to get started. The next thing I needed, which I realised after many calls with consultants and placements was – I needed ready training content. What do you think I did?

I called all the friends from the industry who had any connection with training – and asked them to send me all that they had. In a few hours, my generous friends sent in amazing presentations and a lot of content.

I still remember - by the end of that week, after Googling and friends' support, I had a copious amount of content in my special training hard drive. I am not exaggerating - it must have been definitely more than 100 GB! All of this got me a lot of gigs, and I was a busy freelance trainer. It didn't take long for all this excitement to wear off and for monotony to set in. The thrill was gone.

I began wondering if something was wrong with me. Why could I not stick to one thing? After introspection and a lot of contemplation, I realised two things:

1. I am very passionate about training. It pumps me up and keeps me going.

2. I am not real. I am not giving my 100%. I am using stuff readily available. It is not my stuff – hence it doesn't work for me.

Now, I had to do something about it. *"Action is the foundational key to all success."* ~ Pablo Picasso

I took a week off and designed my own content. Something that I believed in; it was not perfect – but it was me. After that, any piece of training I did was soulful. I was loved and called for more work. I had repeat clients. Some companies even booked me for months at a stretch. If you are thinking I was financially supported during this entire phase, you are wrong! I had rents to pay – both for my parent's and my place; I had my own loans and expenses and I was also planning to get married the same year. So, it was not easy but it was a deliberate choice. It was about being true to myself.

One of the lessons I have learnt in the long run is to Be Yourself. Being anybody else is exhausting. This lesson did not end up being a one time lesson. It's all about how we take the learnings and apply them to different areas of our lives; if you don't, life puts you through similar situations till you learn it.

As you all know, during my journey of becoming a certified coach I moved country. With that move, I was pretty much back to square one. New country, new profile and looking for new clients.

What do you think I did? I did the same thing. I booked a call with every coach online who was offering a free session. I made notes and picked everything they sent me in their emails, I wrapped it under a new cover and offered it as mine. Coaching, however, is not as forgiving a business as training was. I failed royally. I had no new paid clients. I had an awesome looking website, beautifully crafted packages and great profile pictures – but no real paying clients.

Does the above 'me' sound like you?

Today, when I see most coaches doing the same thing, i.e. connecting with other coaches, copying their packages, plans and motto - it hurts. It hurts as these are the coaches who give up on their journey as coaches the soonest.

It did not take me long to realise I was repeating my own history.

What's so fascinating and frustrating and great about life is that you're constantly starting over, all the time, and I love that.- Billy Crystal

I brushed off all the bitterness of everything not working and decided to make things work for me. Dr. Brons words from the coaching study material popped up – crystal clear – I could read it as clear as if it were right in front of me. – "Each individual is whole and complete, and is able to find their own perfect solutions."

Once you tap into yourself – you will see how beautifully creativity just flows out of you. All the wisdom, knowledge, learnings and experience – come together to create a perfectly baked recipe for you.

In no time I came up with my own signature program – Right to Abundance and changed my site from transformationalcoachlife.com to my name – snehalrsingh.com.

This phase of me letting go of my inhibitions and short comings to accepting that I am a creative, capable and wise soul was nothing but a lesson from the Universe.

The lesson was – Be You!! You have all it takes. You've got to work for it though.

I believe that if you want to be successful in your life, you've got to act like a successful person.

I believe that each one of you has what it takes to be successful. The bigger question is - are you doing what it takes to be successful? Yes, manifestation works but, even that needs work.

What does it mean to be successful?

Each one of us has various definitions of success, and each one of us is right. We all are different and have different goals.

Robin Sharma says, if you want to be successful – do what successful people do.

For me success is feeling happy and content, being abundant and having a life filled with love. Each time I get to touch someone's life, I feel fulfilled.

What is your definition of success? What are you doing to be successful? How are you working towards your success? Every small step counts.

Having a system and 'rituals' helps us move faster in the right direction. I have mine - do you have yours?

I connect with what Robin Sharma says -

"Within you lies the sun, the moon, the sky and all the wonders of this universe. The intelligence that created these wonders is the same force that created you. All things around you come from the same source. We are all one. Every being on this Earth, every object on this Earth has a

soul. All souls flow into one, this is the Soul of the Universe. You see, John, when you nourish your own mind and your own spirit, you are really feeding the Soul of the Universe. When you improve yourself, you are improving the lives of all those around you. And when you have the courage to advance confidently in the direction of your dreams, you begin to draw upon the power of the universe. As I told you earlier, life gives you what you ask of it. It is always listening."

I'm listing a few 'must-dos' that have helped me. These are the ones I strongly recommend, so wire it up in your system.

1. **Morning Ritual:** Starting the day right. As per one HuffPost - Richard Branson and Jack Dorsey aren't the only successful people who wake up before the sun.

   In his five-year study of 177 self-made millionaires, author Thomas C. Corley found that nearly 50% of them woke up at least three hours before their workday actually began. Until I challenged myself to wake up early and make it a habit, I got to admit – it was easier said than done. I am a night owl, all my creativity flows in only at night. Since I started waking up at five a.m., I have learnt the power of morning quiet time and its rituals.

2. **Sweat It Out.** The way you begin each day sets up your day. You want to be unstoppable in life, you want to start with at least a 20 - min work out. When you sweat you release BDNF – Brain Derived Neurotrophic Factor – that repairs brain cells from stress. It increases your metabolic rate which gives you energy. Energy is more valuable than even intelligence.

3. **The ABC Hours** – The things that you schedule are the things that get done. There is something really powerful about taking that piece of paper and writing that how your week is going to map out. But I am talking specifics and detail – with social media on rise, most of us spend the free moments of our day tiring our thumbs and scrolling up the phone. So when you map or plan

your week, keep aside everyday for ABC – Assigned Bubble of Concentration and dedicate it to one task that you would do, completely disconnected with the materialistic world. You can dedicate it to your next book, a project, meditation, journaling or anything you want – a complete 'your time'. Block it for family dinners or a walk or anything - anything that would be soulful time for you.

4. **SSS** – Silence-Solitude-Stillness. Spend some time everyday or at least once a week in solitude. Just to think and reflect about how you are living, how you are working, if your daily behavior is aligned with your deepest values. Thinking and reflecting on what you want your legacy to be.

5. **Stay Truly Inspired.** We are all craftsmen and creating a craft in some area of our lives which impacts others we come in touch with. Any game changer legendary epic people did what they did and created what they wanted to create because they were inspired. Protect your inspiration.

   a. Keep it rolling. There is great value in just getting out there and staying energized. Travel – see the world, meet new people – get new energy, new insights.

   b. Breathe the fresh air. Go out and connect with nature. Yes I know you go to the gym and work it out. But once in a while – walk on the grass, feel the soil and fresh air.

   c. Listen to audiobooks, meditation music, music that soothes you. You can do that while taking that walk in nature.

Awareness is the beginning of transformation. While you are doing all the above or even trying out a few things, do not forget to be you. Your education and certifications and life lessons give you the science of how to function in this world; however, you are the art. You are here to serve a purpose and add your flavor to the world.

Being like someone else is easy. Following role models and icon is also easy – they have a path crafted for you. Is it your path? Is this what will make you happy & content?

You know what your path and purpose is deep down. Listen to your inner voice and follow your heart. The idea may sound weird at the start but all great ideas were first called crazy. I believe that in this world , as one of my coach says, 'Crazy People Succeed'. So be Crazy – Live your fullest and be You. You will have so much to give the world then.

Until next time – May anything and everything you do, be done with Love, Grace and Gratitude.

Snehal R. Singh

3x Best-Selling Author, Certified Holistic Business Coach, Writer's Coach,
Publisher & Founder Mind Spirit Works,
Creator of Multiple Book Series including – Coach Wisdom,
International Keynote Speaker

Snehal wears multiple hats – author, publisher, coach and speaker. She has mentored and coached more than 25 Certified Coaches establish their business of coaching and grow 3X through her program – Right to Abundance. (www.righttoabundance.com). She was also nominated for top 30 coaches in USA in 2019. Snehal has trained more than 1000 coaches get certified as an ICF approved Coach.

In 2019, Snehal completed her mission of helping 100 authors – write – publish – flourish. Her Signature Program - Be an Authorpreneur is a complete guide to Write your first book, publish it and grow. She has helped more than 18 authors complete their first book in 2019. Her clients come from all parts of the world – USA, UK, Canada, India, Australia, Cameroon, Nigeria, UAE, Malaysia, Thailand, Germany, France and more.

Snehal's best-selling book "*I Work for Me*" is loved and appreciated by entrepreneurs & Coaches. If you want a copy of her next book-"*An Essence of Soul- The Art of Serving & Mindful Cooking*" absolutely free – email her the receipt of the purchase/transaction ID of this book to info@snehalrsingh.com

If you are looking to expand your business and voice your message through a book or writing – Connect with Snehal now – Book an Appointment

www.snehalrsingh.com

Facebook – Instagram- LinkedIn – Youtube - @snehalauthorpreneur

8

How Psychology & Structure Strengthen Your Coaching

By BJ Radomski

Over the past 20 years I have coached business leaders from around the globe.

In those two decades I've had the great fortune of learning from the greatest coaching minds in the business as well as from the thousands of clients I have had the good fortune to coach.

The coaching models I saw others teach include the GROW model, SCORE model, LEAD model, PRACTICE model, OSKAR model and many more.

What became glaringly apparent to me, is that most of the coaching methodologies I saw were a bit thin in creating the level of results my clients expected.

A common thread these models shared is that they do an acceptable job at surfacing the client's goal. After all, if your conversation is not goal based that's not coaching, it's just a conversation.

From the goal, you then coach to bridge the gap. Ultimately you wrap up your coaching conversation with some sort of commitment steps or action plan. Many of these models also have a strong ending where the coach and client list the committed action steps.

While all these listed coaching models provide a methodology for structuring a conversation, my observation is that they were missing some critical components.

This led me to develop the 6C Coaching Methodology ™. This article hardly provides the space to explain the model in its entirety, but I want to share with you a couple of components that you can add to your coaching methodology.

The following are two ideas taken from the 6C Coaching Model ™.

I found by using these two pieces in my coaching, the client's motivation and follow-up action/s elevate to a much higher level.

These are not "Cut & paste" scripts to read aloud to each client and expect miracles.

You are a trained coach; you can best determine where to weave these approaches into your current model.

If you are not a trained coach or are unsure about how to apply these two questions sets, I invite you to reach out to me personally for support.

The two pieces are around motivation and action planning.

Motivation - The Big Why;

In my early days as a coach I branded myself as a kick-in-the-butt coach. In fact, my first website had this statement "97% of people who meet me don't like me and you probably won't either – but if you want a coach to push you to another level of success – I am the coach for you". Yikes!

The business results were brilliant. My practice was booked solid as I marketed my services to technology start-ups all wanting to be the next internet darling.

What was less pleasant were the results. I coached many clients to successfully achieve goals they didn't necessarily want. They all thought they wanted a goal when they came to me and so I eagerly (and aggressively) coached them to achieve it. What was missing was a proper quality control to be sure that the outcome was indeed what they wanted.

This added process of quality control is the key to their truest motivation.

The benefit of the identified motivation is twofold.

First, we must have fully confirmed that the goal we are working on for the client is indeed the most important thing for them to spend their time on. Often a client will arrive with a goal that is not truly a motivational goal, but just a "nice to have" or a societal inspired pressure in reaction to a clever marketing gimmick.

With the absence of pure motivation, the client will fail to execute the steps required for success, or they may take the steps and successfully achieve the goal only to discover it is not something they truly want.

How do you confirm the goal the client presented is really a goal they want?

Confirming a goal draws upon the two primary motivations - intrinsic and extrinsic.

Clarifying these motivations is done quite simply. We will apply the intrinsic & extrinsic test to both the 'towards' and 'away' motivations.

The question structure to help identify the motivation is:

1) What will you get when you achieve the goal? (extrinsic)

2) What will that get you? (extrinsic)

3) What does that mean to you? (intrinsic)

4) Why is that important? (intrinsic)

What we learn from the following example is that the extrinsic result is not highly motivational.

A recent conversation with a client uncovered the following motivation chain:

"I want to develop my team so they can perform better; so they can achieve the KPI's; so we can all receive the bonus and with the bonus I can get a new car. With a new car I get safety for my children. What's important about this goal is I want my children to be safe."

We then repeat the same series of questions but only in changing the direction. In the second sequence we uncover what will happen if the client does not achieve the goal. The first result will again probably be extrinsic and the rest of the questioning sequence will lead the client to what is most intrinsically important.

You will determine how many times to ask each of the questions to create the richest motivational chain for your client. This is not a formulaic script, rather it is a conceptual process with directional guidelines.

This process creates two driving forces; the 'towards' motivation to achieve the goal and the 'away' motivation which is the pain if we do not achieve the goal. Some clients are driven more by the 'towards' motivation and for others the 'away' motivation is stronger. Both motivations together are the strongest.

An abbreviated version of this sequence are these four simple questions:

1. What benefits will you receive when reaching this goal?

2. Why is that valuable to you?

3. What would happen if you did not reach this goal?

4. Why is that important to you?

The higher your skill in rapport and calibrating, the higher and more meaningful you make these questions. The intrinsic questions can use the phrases; why is that valuable, why is that important, what does it mean to you, what do you believe about this, who will you be when this happens etc.

My invitation to you is to add to this question set after you have clearly determined the desired goal. From these questions you can determine if the goal is a "nice to have", a "spontaneous whim", or a truly meaningful goal with enough desire to provide the needed motivation to achieve.

Execution – The Action Plan

You have now identified the goal and beautifully articulated the motivations to achieve it.

The next requirement is to determine the action steps. Many new coaches have shared with me their temptation to give advice rather than coach the client to their own solution. After a bit of questioning I usually discover it is due to the quality of questions offered to the client. Many coaches feel high pressured to perform, so in the absence of a client-offered solution, the coach will provide their own.

This section includes four different questioning directions to support the client in creating a solution on their own.

The four directions are:

i.   what do you know?

ii. what do you remember?

iii. what do you imagine? and

iv. what can we brainstorm?

Each direction serves a purpose and supports the client in navigating all their mental capacities.

The first step is the simplest. By asking "So, what do you think you can do?" we are appealing to the intellectual or rational part of the brain.

In many cases after having clearly articulating the exact detail of the goal and highlighting the motivations, your client may be able to rationally come up with the required action steps.

It would be lovely if this happened all the time.

Instead, what often happens is, the client is unable to surface a solution. Instead, stress surfaces. The client may begin to doubt their intelligence, skills, knowledge, experience or ability to achieve the goal. This pressure of not being able to find a solution can result in an emotional state that is not resourceful. As more cortisol or adrenalin enters the blood system the access to rational and clear thinking diminishes. You can see how this spirals in a negative way.

When this happens, we want to interrupt the process and go to a more resourceful plan.

When the client does not have an answer, we interrupt this direction of thinking and shift to memory.

The coach now asks the question "have you ever had anything similar, maybe back in school maybe in another job?"

This is a great question because the coach is not asking them to solve a problem with a right or wrong answer. We are just asking for a memory where there are no wrong answers. Think of it like asking someone what is $131 * 27$ which requires calculation as compared to asking for their telephone number.

This second question allows our client to go through their memory banks, scour around and search for something they can bring to the surface that may have a transferable skill or action to apply on this new goal. This is not stressful; it's simply repeating a memory.

If a client is still unable to come up with an answer, we activate another part of the brain with our next question.

Moving away from rational thinking and memory, we go to the creative by asking a question which would be impossible for them to know and not something they could remember.

The structure of the imagination question is to apply the same situation to a well-known person.

An example could be "What do you think Elon Musk would have done if he had this same issue?"

Of course, your client could never know and we reassure them nobody could know.

The purpose of this question design is to give freedom to offer ideas with no fear of judgement.

Lastly, if we want more options the coach could then ask if the client wants a brainstorming session.

The suggested model for this sequence is for the coach to begin by suggesting a few silly or unrealistic ideas to get the brainstorm started and the creativity flowing.

 From the generated list, the coach then asks the client which idea they would like to start with.

This four-step process allows the client to access separate brain functions and provide a rich list of options to choose from.

By inserting these two sections into your existing coaching model you will enrich the quality of your coaching. To discuss this in greater detail I invite you to send me an email at BJ@bjradomski.com and I would be pleased to answer any other questions you may have relating to this.

BJ Radomski

Executive Coach, Licensed Neuro-Semantic Trainer, Co-founder - The Coach Training Academy

Executive coach Brian (BJ) Radomski is a bottom line driven professional and has been running his own successful coaching practice for over 10 years. As one of the early adopters in the coaching industry, BJ has been called upon by many new coaches to improve their skills and assist them with establishing a practice.

Over the last several years in Asia, BJ has focused on bringing life coach training certification programs of the highest quality into organizations. His workshops have been training managers, executives and business owners how to become internal coaches and transform their organizations.

BJ is thrilled to join Master Coach Steve Kiges and offer long-distance life coach training certification and the elite coach training through The Coach Training Academy.

In addition to his coaching practice (www.BJRadomski.com) BJ has owned and operated businesses in North America and Asia.

Working with BJ, you learn coaching is not just about theory.

9

A Woven History: Called To Lead

BY PIPER HARRIS

D on't you love a story? I do. I relish the stories you will read in this chapter. Each and every one are the clients and individuals I have encountered over my 20 years of experience. All of these women have molded me into who I am today. When I started my journey, I had copious amounts of traditional learning from my college years to certifications as well as various professions. All the facts were helpful but I still found myself lost;

HOW do I actually apply this? WHAT will I be faced with?

My hope in sharing stories is that

- it will allow you to visualize different client needs,
- it will give various scenarios I have faced as a coach,
- it will introduce you to new tools you can apply in your coaching practice, and
- it will help you in confidently determining your coaching vision and niche, to move forward in this exciting profession you have chosen!

***

Listen: A Personal Story

The sun was shining so brightly, I squinted into it, as I approached the most sacred swing, coveted by all on the playground. I climbed onto the swing and tightly grasped the metal. I pumped my legs, harder and harder, each time feeling my stomach drop as I swung up and then I floated momentarily, suspended weightlessly in the clouds, only to fall back onto the swing, and pump harder and harder.

Then, someone caught my eye. She was small with brownish blonde frizzy hair. She sat on the concrete ledge, her back to me, her shoulders slumped. I could see the slightest tremble escape from her. I slowed my pumping legs, heeding the voice in my heart quietly saying, "Go."

I heard my calling in 1986. Yes, I was only 7 years old. The internal voice I heard say "Go" began a lifelong journey of coaching women and women-led organizations to fully embrace success and leadership.

Application Opportunity

Identify Your Call. What is it telling you? You must identify to whom you will serve. A broad application without a deep understanding as to why and who you choose to coach can lead quickly to burn out. Who is your client, what is their age, what is their education level, what do they read, watch, or listen to? What are their pain points? What do you want to inspire in them? This will allow you to hone in on the person you will serve, leading them diligently in a focused approach.

***

Filtering Thoughts: A Client's Story

It was lights out. I was exhausted by multiple intakes, counselors calling in sick, and an outbreak of lice. Was it a full moon?! The house was rattling with tension. I opened the last door to bid the tenants goodnight, her bright blue eyes lit up in the dark, "Will you talk to me?" After small chatter, she quietly sobbed: "I will never get there."

My Story

Lying or truthful thoughts. I worked in applied developmental psychology with a focus on child and adolescent development. This led me to years working in group homes and psychiatric units. The tears I shared with the young clients broke my heart and had me grappling with thoughts of "Am I good enough?" "Can I actually do this?" As a coach, you will battle these same thoughts that work to deny your call to coaching.

Application Opportunity

Filter Truth From Lies. Recognize that lies will be wedged between your fears. The most common opponent you will face is Imposter Syndrome. The common links are emotions entrenched in fear of failure or of the unknown, and the need for perfection. Some of these thoughts include "never" and "always". The feeling of being a fraud or questioning if you will ever succeed, can be paralyzing. Rather than be fearful and retreat, recognize this voice, filter what is TRUTH or LIE. Will, you truly "never" reach something, will you "always" feel a certain way? Then, break down the job or goal you are faced with into small steps. Ask yourself, when the Imposter rises, is this based on reality or emotion? Work to achieve each small step which builds you up as a coach in tangible truths and realized goals.

***

Finding Balance: A Client's Story

Exhausted and hopeless, she had tried everything from typical treatments to others on the fringe of mainstream medicine. Hundreds of thousands of dollars spent in hopes of giving her son a better life. His disorder ravaged him, she watched his battle while juggling her own. She was running her family's multimillion-dollar company, learning the ropes in order to step into the CEO role when her father retired. Apart from that, she hosted weekly networking events and wrote monthly articles for the local paper. She was being pulled in too many directions. Her eyes welled with tears but the smell from the kitchen drew her in swiftly; she quietly spoke, "When will I find balance?"

My Story

Out of balance. I was a private chef and nutrition coach. I had two children under the age of three begging for my attention, I was working to write a cookbook, gaining multiple nutritionist certifications, managing my clientele, and dreaming of finding stardom on national cooking shows. Not only do our clients fall out of balance, but you will too. You will see flashy ads telling you how to build out a new website, pay exorbitant amounts of money guaranteeing clients, your ego will push you to take just one more call, just one more client, all at the cost of your personal wellness and the neglect of those around you.

Application Opportunity

Create Space. Coaching can lead to hour creep. You must create space by applying the blocking method. Block the hours in your week for 1) coaching clients 2) accounting 3) marketing efforts 4) professional development/networking 5) self/family and 6) "white space." Knowing exactly what is ahead of you by simply adding specific blocks to your calendar will keep you on task. Guard your "white space". This is time to sit quietly, to reflect. You need this time to recharge and continue in the creative and gratifying process as a coach.

***

Learn: A Personal Story

She was beautiful. She stood tall amongst the women, with long, thick brown hair, tanned skin, and a smile you could see a mile away. She was humble and graceful. Having a dreamer's imagination and the refined skill of a strategist, she worked tirelessly in creating a difference. She spoke multiple languages, skillfully made connections, and sought to better herself and those around her. She listened intently while also drawing out answers through thoughtful conversations, "You have to really listen. What are they really saying; what aren't they saying? I know YOU want this, what makes you so on fire for this?"

My Story

Learning from my mentor made an indelible mark in my life. To this day I remember moments with her that keep me centered and moving toward my calling as a coach. Coaching can be exhausting and create a lot of questions. In these seasons of your career, you will need an advocate, someone to lean on and learn from.

Application Opportunity

Find A Mentor. This is key to your success, though finding a mentor isn't always the easiest. Search out groups where you can meet others and understand that you may not find a singular mentor. However, if you are keenly aware of those around you, you will glean valuable information. Get involved with groups like business networks, ICF chapters, old classmates/professors, LinkedIn groups, churches, and more. And remember, when others feed into you, you also have the opportunity to feed into others - you too can be a mentor.

***

Stand Firm: A Client Story

She came into the session with strength and resilience - something I had seen in her over many years, but this time something was different. She was hurt and angered; however, she was energized. The feelings of disrespect were immense but her deep desire to pursue her creativity in authentic leadership overrode the waves of negativity. "I'm being cut off at the knees; they don't see my vision nor do they want to hear me out. They keep telling me I can't do it. They're wrong... This is what I have been called to do."

My Story

Resistance. I had every platform filled to the brim with ads, creative content and copy, and various markets I was pursuing. I was exhausted having to run my business while raising children and keeping my home, but I was determined to forge through. Upon opening an email to begin my day, I saw it *"Questions: Why Won't You Coach Me - Who Do You think You Are?!"* "Oh no. What was this about? Do I have to *open* this?"

This was the first time I encountered true resistance to my chosen niche, women and women-led organizations, *only*. The gentleman berated my choice of niche, demeaned my efforts in effecting change in women's lives, and promised demise would come to my coaching practice. That was three years ago.

Application Opportunity

Confidence. Just like my client who was feeling resistance in her position while also wanting to pursue her path, I too have felt resistance in my coaching practice. You can choose to accommodate every demographic possible; however, ask yourself - does every population speak to your true mission and vision for your practice? If your answer is yes, how so? What are the common themes? If you answered no, it's time to confidently choose with whom you will coach.

I have chosen to work solely with women and women-led organizations for a variety of specific reasons:

1. I understand being a woman (the most obvious of reasons!)
2. I feel women face different expectations of roles than men i.e. being the sole homemaker/child caregiver
3. I feel there is an enormous gap in equal leadership opportunities for women
4. I want to empower women to lead successful lives, whether they are a stay – at - home mom, Solopreneur, or CEO. I believe each woman is called to lead and I want to see that developed in every woman I meet.

This takes confidence. I stand firm in my coaching call. Understand, you are choosing to be a professional coach, which also means you choose whom you coach. Stand firm in your beliefs. If you're a man who ONLY wants to coach men, great! WHY? If you're a woman who ONLY wants to coach abuse victims, great! Why? If you're a man who ONLY wants to coach female top executives in tech, great? Why? If you're a woman who ONLY wants to coach LGBTQ, great! Why?

It takes confidence to stand in your choice and rest assured, you will feel and see resistance. You will question if you're cutting yourself off from a more abundant income, you will question your choice when someone inevitably responds negatively. Standing firm in your chosen niche and approach is foundational in creating longevity in your career.

***

Perseverance: A Client's Story

She arrived bleary-eyed to the 5am session with the other women, fair-skinned and a welcoming smile. She worked hard, sweat poured as she fixed her jaw and fought through the discomfort. She carried a heaviness. Yes, she was searching for physical confidence but there was something else. I placed my hand on her left side, "Watch that hip, focus where your knee follows, take it slower." She erupted into tears fleeing outside. An hour later she emerged, "I can't bear this anymore! After he died I lost all hope, all confidence - I keep going, but it's so hard."

My Story

Keep moving. This couldn't be happening. I invested so much of myself. 60 hour weeks, my heart and soul, I thought for sure this was the perfect opportunity to affect hundreds of lives. But, they didn't see it that way. I was done. Then the phone rang, "We see something in the image, we need to do a biopsy." In just 10 days, I had lost what I thought was the perfect coaching position, said goodbye to my beloved clients, and was told I may have breast cancer.

Application Opportunity

Persevere. Just like my client who sought out fitness coaching for physical confidence, who was in the midst of enormous pain from losing her husband but kept fighting forward, you too will be faced with pain, fear, and loss as I was. Perseverance isn't just something we coach our clients through, you will need to keep a tight hold on tenacity and grit when life throws you situations you aren't prepared for. *Action begets action.* Reflect and recall situations where you forged through critical times in your life and came out on top. Focus on this and use it to brighten your path when all seems shrouded in darkness.

***

Grow: A Client's Story

She stomped and paced back and forth. Sick and tired of the sleepy little town, chained to the ideals of others, pigeonholed into what she should be and do, she had had enough. Frustrated and ready to escape she knew she had to think clearly, "I just can't figure it out, I want out of here. I want to leave. I need a new career!"

My Story

Opportunities will arise to grow in your profession. Through 20 years of work I have my Bachelor's in psychology, was a certified mental health counselor, private chef, certified nutritionist, author, business owner, certified personal trainer, fitness studio owner, wife, mom, certified life coach, and certified organizational development coach.

Application Opportunity

Professionalism. You made the decision to become a coach; however, in that, it's important to continue to grow in your profession, seeking out certifications and credentialing is key to be a step above the rest. Invest in networking groups and continued education. Ensure you are at the top of the coaching field and fine-tune your techniques and skills.

And remember, different positions will each give you the skills you need to develop your unique coaching style.

***

Woven History

Many times I have wondered if I truly heard the call to develop women leaders. My professions didn't seem to connect. I second-guessed my training and how I could apply it. The most helpful tools I have learned along the way have been to embrace my calling in every situation, identify my niche, filter truth from lies when the Imposter Syndrome kicks in, recognize the need for a blocked calendar to maintain balance personally and professionally, embracing the lifeline a mentor truly is, stand in confidence in my coaching path, the need for grit to persevere, and continued professional development. You see, now I recognize each position built on another. Each client's story mirrored much of mine. Had I not experienced those different opportunities I would not have deeply developed my call to lead women.

Entering into coaching can coax out insecurities in you. Remember, each client and each experience is building you as a coach. Books and certifications are wonderful tools, but if you listen carefully to your story, develop your why in the pursuit of being a coach, explore the people and opportunities you encounter, you will hear something. A richly woven history with exactly the tools and talents you'll need to heed your call to lead.

Piper Harris

Author & Women's Success Coach - Empowering midlevel women leaders in accelerated clarity & design of personal & professional achievement

Piper Harris is the CEO and Coach of Poiema Women's Success Coaching for individual women and women-led organizations, published author of 4 books, business owner, wife, and mom. Piper has worked with people development and success coaching for over 15 years ranging from mental health counseling, program  management, and community mobilization. While also growing thriving businesses as a solopreneur, mentoring of other women-driven business, and living an abundant life as a wife and mom.

Facebook – Twitter- poiemacoaching

Instagram – LinkedIn: poiemawomenscoaching

10

Self-Full Caring

DR. ARAVINDAN RAGHAVAN

I n this chapter I would like to share my journey : the journey of how coaching transformed me; the journey of self - discovery and an evolved niche coaching style; and the journey of applying this style as a life and executive coach in the field of excellence to reform many organizations.

I Surrendered to coaches and their wisdom which got me that memorable self-discovery day

It all started when I was nominated for Executive leadership coaching with a team of global coaches conducting a residential program for foundations of great leadership, in phases on topics such as Authenticity, Integrity, Being cause in the matter, and Being Committed to Something Bigger than Oneself.

This program included topics covering self - transformation, leadership development techniques and setting up context in life. One to one coaching session were planned beautifully after every phase of the topics so as to enhance leadership capabilities through self - discovery and to work on improvement. Along the way, my intuition indicated that this was a golden opportunity in life to get transformed to a better leader so I decided to surrender completely to the coaches without any ego or judgments in mind.

That really worked very well for me - to explore in depth about myself along with the coach through transparent discussions conducted with mutual trust and relationship. In fact, one particular time the coach was becoming more enthusiastic than me when she saw that my efforts and actions towards achieving the focus goals which were committed during each coaching session, were bearing fruition. Once I started implementing that directly in home & work area environment, I could easily feel the transformation in me and it was validated when my wife, boss, peers, sub ordinates, and all other colleagues experienced the difference. During the end of the coaching, all were asked to set context in life based on our own values, beliefs and parameters which has thus far laid the road of success and we were asked to think it over the entire night and present it the next day. When reflecting upon it and spending hours thinking, I finally found my life context was the Self-Full Caring™ life context and there were a lot of goose bumps when I presented this to the whole team of coaches and members of the program.

It was at that juncture that I felt the day had arrived; my life's purpose and how to use it for the benefit of others. This one 'Aha' moment made me understand the power of having a coach, the wisdom of coaching and its Self-full experience.

The other biggest compliment came when I successfully managed to integrate my Self-Full Caring™ principles in my organization role as Excellence leader to lead self, others and business effectively and finally evolved as a Self-Full Caring™ coach.

As a certified life and executive coach with ACC level mentoring towards ICF –ACC level credentials today. I am proud to have created a complete package in my niche area - Self-Full Caring™ coaching delivers to any organization, an integrated approach to excellence leadership credential levels like black belt and master black belt.

Your Original Niche Area Makes You Special

Many words such as self-full, self-love, self-care are available on the meaning of loving yourself first before others and focusing on a one dimension view. My niche area of coaching, Self-Full Caring™, is a multi-dimensional impactful word and to me it is caring the self, the family, the team, the organization and society in full; and for that to happen you need to transform within, to be whole and complete. Self-Full Caring™ shows the mark of excellence and effective leadership qualities.

As an experienced coach , I was successfully able to integrate with the excellence areas of the lean six sigma, to deploy the strategy execution by transforming individuals **(Self)**, building effective cross functional teams **(Others)**, having stakeholder centered coaching and also working closely with executives to create value to business **(Organization)**.

All the principles of coaching like active listening, power questioning and motivating were used and seeing the teams achieve their own creative solution in their respective work areas was gratifying. I also conduct 1:1 coaching sessions for management and managers in an effort for them to express their goals and remove barriers in their minds and work place, so as to work with open minds and without negativity or judgments.

Seven phases: Transform, Perform, Reform

As a Self-Full Caring™ coach, I recommend seven phases to follow to become an excellence leader.

1. **UNDERSTAND**
2. **TRANSFORM**
3. **BUILD**
4. **PRACTICE**
5. **POSITION**
6. **BRAND**
7. **APPLY**

The critical step of Transform is done using a unique **PERFECT™** coaching formula. All the above seven steps will be published in detail in my upcoming books entitled Self-Full Caring™ (focusing on three editions one by one Part *1* -Transform, *Part 2*- Perform, *Part 3*- Reform)

Integrating Coaching Principles In All Areas of Life and Work

Currently I am practicing and applying ™in the organization where I'm currently employed as a leadership coach role to create more excellence leaders in the organization. In an organization, as is in life, every individual needs to show niche skills along with routine work to be successful, grow faster and get recognition. Acquisition of skills through knowledge or training is in plentiful supply nowadays (Online or classroom) but leading oneself with the right mindset, having confidence in life and in the work place are keys to success for that individual. So, it is necessary to transform an individual into an Excellence leader first and then nurture the seed of all the skills which will mature and enhance him / her to apply effectively and consistently positive thinking and confidence as the situations demand it.

Creating more excellence leaders is also needed due to business competitiveness and growth. As an organization excellence leader for more than the last 10 years and working in various corporations, I realized that organizations are missing out on a great opportunity of asset creation if they do not transform managers into excellence leaders. Most organizations employ consultants to bring cultural change and transformation which is normally short lived whereas the organizations which have transformed many employees through coaches, have been able to create a huge long term value -add. Even the individuals should realize that by transforming themselves to excellence leader they can have great career growth and leadership positions. As a Self-Full Caring™ coach, I am able to demystify the excellence leadership curriculum of master black belt of American Society of Quality(www.asq.org) to an interesting coaching program along with core competencies of coaching integrated with excellence skills and strategies.

Transform leaders: Unlock Potential to Lock value

Self-Full Caring™ is designed for individuals to Unlock potential to Lock value permanently, and to Transform from Manager level to an Excellence Leader level. An Excellence leader is a person who has leadership qualities along with excellence skills (covering simple lean six sigma methodology. tools, techniques) who can manage both life and work efficiently and effectively. Leadership is achieved when one balances the body, emotions and language in difficult situations to lead self, teams and organization. In many companies even though there are many people with skills and experiences they are limited with adaptive skills of leadership which prevent them from growing to higher positions. The factor which is preventing them is not the capability but the ignorance of understanding that the limitations arise from themselves.

By executive leadership coaching, organizations can transform many managers to excellence leaders who can support the organizational excellence journey faster and be sustainable. In many companies we have seen coaching needs arise from CEO level to manager levels as the limitations can be unique in nature, as it is specific to the person - something which the coach can recognize through assessment, powerful questioning and the coaching process. The self-awareness and performing to maximum potential will create significant lifetime value for individuals personally and professionally.

The journey of an individual to an excellence leader will be through a coach who can nurture the leadership qualities using the 360 Degree Assessment, i.e. analyzing strengths and weaknesses, focusing on techniques to overcome the mind barriers, as well as interferences which are limiting their capability. By making individuals understand the voice of fear, the voice of cynicism, and the voice of judgment, we can transform an individual to a better leader through structured coaching and guiding to see the way forward.

To transform a manager to a leader, we need to break the icebergs (mind blocks) caused due to life sentences, hard beliefs and make them focus on mindfulness and achieve higher emotional quotient (EQ). As an excellence corporate leader and Self-Full Caring™ coach I would like to cover in detail all the above topics and the stories of such transformation which have happened for many individuals in my upcoming books and articles on Self-Full Caring™ using the unique coaching **PERFECT**™ formula.

Concluding with a famous Chinese proverb that is apt for the Self-Full Caring™ coach -

"If you want one year of prosperity, grow grain.

If you want ten years of prosperity, grow trees.

If you want one hundred years of prosperity, grow people."

DR. Aravindan Raghavan

Corporate Head- Global Operational Excellence
– Syngene International Ltd,

Excellence Leadership Coach, Master Black belt, International accredited Lean Six sigma trainer, an Author and an International Public Speaker.

He is an engineer with B. Tech Chemical. He has also studied General Management from Indian School of Business. He has trained 8200+ employees globally

His 25 years of experience in Petrochemical, Pharma sectors makes him an expert in managing Global Operational Excellence, Supply chain management in Big Pharma companies at corporate level. He has a unique experience of deployment of operational excellence program to entire pharma value chain business verticals ranging from Research services, API. formulations, Biologics to achieve mastery. He has won multiple national awards and recognitions for best six sigma projects, Awarded Level 3 Qualitist by Qimpro and Six sigma professional of the year 2018 in manufacturing supply chain for contributions to pharma industry in field of excellence.

Aravindan's vision is to touch and influence lives of at least 10000 people by December 2020. He helps in areas excellence and leadership.

www.selffullcaring.com

https://www.linkedin.com/in/aravindan69/

Email - aravind69@yahoo.com

11

Metamorphosis: Becoming a Transformational Leader

BY PRIYANKA SINHA

The biological process in which an organism, particularly a butterfly goes through the life cycle, involving it in developing from eggs into larvae, larvae growing into pupae which finally becomes a vivacious, adult butterfly is known as metamorphosis. The analogy of a transforming butterfly resonates well with my personal journey of evolution into becoming a resourceful transformational leader. Coach Wisdom, Volume 2 serves as a unique platform through which I intend to position myself as a transformational leader in the coaching industry. I am going to showcase some of my valuable competencies and unique capabilities in the ensuing paragraphs. Some of the key areas in my expertise include my vocational profile as a certified life coach, published bestselling author, non-dual or awareness guide, recreation and wellness practitioner for older adults, energy healer and budding entrepreneur. These competencies involve engaging with clients in capacities that empower, influence, facilitate, support and provide services that will benefit them, thereby enhancing the quality of their lives, making a positive impact on and influencing them in constructive ways.

Becoming a Certified Life Coach was an endeavor that began when I was able to identify my own need for support and guidance as I decided to transition in my career as a recreation aide towards becoming a self-employed life coach in August 2017. I enrolled in a nine-month certified life coach training program offered online by Symbiosis Coaching, a premier Life Coaching institute which provides ICF approved, convenient Life Coach training programs. After graduating from this program in March 2018, I received my certification as a Certified Personal Transformation Coach (C.P.T.C.) affiliated with the Certified Coaches Alliance. Thereafter, I registered as a life coach with Noomi, an online directory of coaches that offers services for clients online. Taking a step towards becoming a self-employed life coach, I registered my coaching business, known as Stepping Stone Coaching through which I have been and am offering my coaching services for clients online. The niche for my coaching services are in the key areas of fulfilment and personal transformation. The ideal clients that I want to support are those who are relatively self-aware and want to invest in enhancing their level of satisfaction and those who are committed to their personal transformation for up leveling their lives.

In addition to becoming a certified coach, my passion for writing seems to have manifested powerfully through my writing projects so far. One of my first published writing was featured in a workbook for mental health recovery known as Finding My Way: Stories of Recovery published by the Self-help Alliance in 2013. As I started training as a life coach, my writing journey took a turn for the better. I'm pleased to have co-authored an Amazon bestseller in the self-help genre known as Release: Untold Stories about Inner Strength, Resilience and Overcoming Challenges, Volume 2 published by 7 Publishing in 2018. The chapter I wrote sheds light on my personal journey as an energy healer; it is called Blessings of a Wounded Healer.

My third published work is for a book series known as 20 Beautiful Women, Volume 6 that will be published by 7 Publishing shortly. The chapter I have penned is 'Calling of a Rising Soul'- this describes my journey of personal transformation and gives you a glimpse of my purpose as a multidimensional light-bearer. Finally, the latest writing project that I'm working towards is Coach Wisdom, Volume 2 through which I share my journey of evolution and expertise as a transformational leader who wants to make a positive impact and have a transformational influence on my clients and readers.

The third set of competencies that I want to highlight is offered through my role as a non-dual or awareness guide. I'm particularly keen on sharing nondual awareness with my clients by supporting them in accessing and integrating awareness in a space of nondual transmission. This modality is particularly suited to being offered during coaching and facilitation and can be adapted in various settings. My introduction to nondual teachings began with my participation in the Radiant Mind program created by Peter Fenner, PhD. who is a leader in the Western adaptation of Buddhist wisdom. He is a pioneer in the new field of nondual psychotherapy. Radiant Mind is a nine-month program that offers several opportunities for accessing and resting in non-dual awareness in the presence of the guide, participants and coaches. I attended this valuable course with a friend at the University of British Columbia in Vancouver back in 2010. It was overall a profound experience; I definitely want to guide my clients in reaping the benefits of swiftly awakening them to the liberating freedom of nondual awareness.

My personal journey as an energy healer started with my nearly magical initial experience with Reiki or life force energy. A former roommate in my college days in Pune, India offered me a session to ease my bothersome headache. Being convinced of the magic in the energy healing, I decided to get attuned for Reiki Level 1 in Newcastle, U.K. en route to Toronto, Canada as a permanent resident in 2004. In the spring of 2006, I upgraded to Reiki Level 2 through attunements by a Reiki Master along with a friend. Thereafter, I have offered energy healing sessions on request from time to time. Having successfully graduated from the Recreation and Leisure Studies program from Conestoga College Institute of Technology and Advanced Learning in 2014, I'm trained as a Recreation Practitioner, offering recreation and wellness programs for residents in retirement and long-term care settings. As I take steps towards becoming a successful entrepreneur, I want to offer my range of skills and expertise in order to bring value and provide innovative solutions to my clients' problems and gradually build my coaching practice. These are the various capacities in which I can serve my clients' needs and demonstrate being an influential transformational leader.

My journey of alchemical transformation can be glimpsed by this illuminating story on the evolution of my consciousness to higher dimensions. The hero-quest within me is marked by the inner calling to find my authentic or soul self. I intend to shed light on certain legs of my journey of personal transformation that I consider worth sharing for the benefit of my future coaching clients and prospective readers. This year (2019) bears witness to my incredible spiritual metamorphosis ever since I began engaging with the complex inner processes of shadow work, inner child healing and soul work during the summer months. The last ten months have been steeped in coping with psychological trauma, processing difficult emotions and struggling to access mental clarity and focus. There were some unavoidable family issues that adversely affected me towards the latter part of last year that led to a downward spiral in my overall psychological health and spiritual wellness. This was a culmination of an internal psychological struggle and emotional pressure buildup that became catalytic and pushed me towards the brink of my transformative descent into the realm of darkness. These challenging and dark experiences marked by spiritual depression have often been experienced by some as an existential crisis, also known as the Dark Night of the Soul. Eckhart Tolle sheds some light on spiritual emergencies along these lines by these words.

"Life will give you whatever experience is most helpful for the evolution of your consciousness. How do you know this is the experience you need? Because this is the experience you are having at this moment."

Soul work is a phenomenal pathway on one's path of spiritual ascension. It involves descending into the core of our beings, removing inner blockages, and undertaking the courageous task of healing, forgiving, understanding, empowering, and loving ourselves. In order to reconnect with the innate wholeness within us, it is vital that we work with our souls. All of life is blessed when you learn to embody the pure unconditional love that is your True Nature. Our dream, vision, and life-calling is to help you fulfill your soul's destiny. The substantial inner work was followed by an awakening of the divine feminine energy, also known as the rise of the goddess energy. This is the energy within us and in the universe that serves life itself. The qualities of unconditional love, compassion, wisdom, beauty, gentleness, patience, accepting, forgiving, nurturing, healing, welcoming, of being accessible, being kind, being intuitive, and so much more, are carried by the Divine Feminine aspect.

This led to gaining a sense of wholeness and spiritual rebirth that graced my entire being as these sacred energies were being integrated within my body-mind. There was a period of rebalancing as the energies flowed within and the chakra system was being activated. Finally, a gradual inner alignment with source energy began taking place. The process was taking place at a deeper cellular level; I sensed my celestial light body (photonic energy) being activated. This inner transformation is directly linked to my soul purpose of walking the light-bearer's path. A light-bearer is a person destined to enlighten the path of others by helping them connect with the divine energy within and the multidimensional aspects to assist them on their soul journey. They carry the divine mission of giving positive guidance as the world goes through a positive shift from the traditional way of living to a world that is more conscious and on a higher vibration.

On my hero's journey, I can visualize myself having been through the first two phases of departure and initiation. I had begun detaching from the ordinary world as I transitioned into hermit mode after trying to cope with mundane struggles and family issues. With the aid of my spirit guides and support network, I mustered the courage to cross the threshold and set forth on my dark and challenging spiritual ordeal. Thereafter, I stepped into the special world of spiritual practice, completed the tests in the presence of my inner allies and foes, continued my spiritual ascension journey, and finally obtained the fruit of inner transformation while discovering my soul mission of service as a "light-bearer". The glorious return to the ordinary world with the divine treasure hasn't manifested yet since the process of integrating higher vibrations is still happening. I would surely want to continue walking the light-bearer's path since my powerful spiritual rebirth. I will endeavor to share my divine gifts of intuitive wisdom, life coaching expertise, nondual guidance, energy healing, alchemical capabilities and authorship for the benefit of my clients and readers.

In today's Era of Technology a.k.a. Digital Age, the internet has most certainly provided us with accessibility to on-demand services, commerce and interactions that are far more complex and it has also glued us to our devices. It is easy to get sidetracked by these distractions which alter our perception of reality, sucking us into the digital ether and leaving us dismayed and beleaguered in our quest to reach our goals. As the connectivity through the web skyrockets for the global population so does the ever-growing distraction. For those wishing and willing to cut through the proverbial noise, life coaching offers a cliched "life hack" or an alternate approach to increased productivity and lessened attention to distractions thereby revolutionizing achieving clients' dreams. Life coaches in the digital age can be instrumental in assisting clients in reaching their goals by holding them accountable and providing guidance as is required by the specific life situation. Likewise, a Certified Life Coach with the specialty niche of personal transformation can skillfully guide and hold clients accountable as they explore and navigate their personal journeys of transformation.

The following are some of the characteristics of transformational leaders.

- Keep their ego in check. ...
- Self-management. ...

- Ability to take the right risks. ...
- Make difficult decisions. ...
- Share collective organizational consciousness. ...
- Inspirational. ...
- Entertain new ideas. ...
- Adaptability

Likewise, my intention as a transformational author is to inspire my readers on their personal journeys through the insights and pointers I offer in a written format. In closing, I want to leave my readers with an inspiring quote that is key to any type of personal transformation.

"If you do follow your bliss, you put yourself on a kind of track that has been there all the while, waiting for you, and the life that you ought to be living is the one you are living. Follow your bliss and don't be afraid, and doors will open where there were no doors before."

~ Joseph Campbell, The Power of Myth

Priyanka Sinha

Certified Personal Transformation Coach (CPTC), Founder of Stepping Stones Coaching, Published Author, Recreation Professional, Awareness Guide, Energy Healer, Vocal Artist and Improvisor

Priyanka has co-authored an Amazon bestseller in the self-help or motivational genre known as Release: Untold Stories About Inner Strength, Resilience and Overcoming Challenges, Vol. 2 published by 7 Publishing in 2018. Thereafter, she has co-authored another book known as 20 Beautiful Women, Vol. 6 in 2019. She is a graduate of the Recreation and Leisure Studies program and the winner of the Rick Casey Courage to Cope Award at Conestoga College Institute of Technology and Advanced Learning in 2014. She has served the older adult population in her community as a Recreation Aide in retirement and long-term care settings. Priyanka Sinha is proud participant of the Radiant Mind program created by Dr. Peter Fenner; she serves in the capacity of a Nondual Awareness Guide, offering nondual awareness sessions for participants on Skype. She is an Energy Healer (Reiki Practitioner) and feels called to fulfill her soul mission of service as a Divine Light-bearer and Soul Alchemist. Priyanka wants to help others connect with the divine energy within and multidimensional aspects thereby providing assistance on their personal soul journeys.

http://www.steppingstones-coaching.weebly.com/

http://linkedin.com/in/priyanka-sinha-c-p-t-c-31546218

Instagram stepping_stones_coaching

12

Changing the World; One Leader, One Coach at a Time

By Nicholas Mattone

In my role at John Mattone Global I have the opportunity to speak with some of the most incredible leaders and coaches across the globe. As the Chief Relationship Officer, I manage our client relationships and sales process. Our company offers three main buckets.

1. John Mattone CEO Executive Coaching

2. John Mattone Speaking/Retreats

3. The Intelligent Leadership Executive Coaching Certification.

Let's focus on #3 because it is the centerpiece of John Mattone Global. We currently have over 550 Coaches that represent over 53 countries across the globe. These coaches are considered a part of our Intelligent Leadership Family. Just over 2 years ago John (My Father) went to the International Coach Federation to apply for his accreditation for our program! Since then we now have 5 additional "Deeper Dive" programs that we can offer our coaches for ongoing learning and ultimately become a Master Level Intelligent Leadership Coach under the John

Mattone brand. Our coaches can receive up to 90 CCE Coaching Credits.

The coaches and leaders that we certify and interact with, come from all different types of backgrounds. They might have been coaching for 30 plus years or they may have just started their career as a coach and have found their passion but need a process and playbook to start their coaching career. We also certify internal coaches who are coaching within their companies such as HR Leaders or executives that are planning on retiring in a couple of years and want to start their coaching career. The relationships I have built and the conversations that I have had over the past few years have been life changing. I am a very social being and enjoy diving deep into how we can help these leaders reach their full potential in life and in their careers. When these leaders and coaches come to us, they are looking for guidance, support, tools and a methodology they can use to help their clients unlock and unleash their full potential.

Each coach is different and has his / her own personality but ultimately as a coach and a leader you need specific tools that sets you apart from your competition. That's why continuing to learn and upskill yourself is one of the most important traits you need, if you are to be successful in anything that you do. When I speak with the coaches who want to learn from John and become certified, the first thing they say is, I want to better myself and want to learn a new process and add additional tools to my toolkit.

What we do is enable these coaches to help leaders and future leaders unlock and unleash their potential so they truly become the best leaders and people they can be. The IL Executive Coaching Process ignites and strengthens a leader's inner-core and outer-core, which enables him / her to realize four (4) "game-changing" outcomes that they can leverage as leaders in their business and lives: altruism, affiliation, achievement, and abundance (The 4 A's). The 4 A's are the seeds to achieving sustained greatness and creating a lasting legacy. We also offer an extensive 600-page Coaches Resource Manual; and while optional, but highly recommended, is the two-year development journey to help the certified IL coach grow their coaching skills as well as enhance their success as a coach.

Post program and certification, some of our coaches have reached amazing heights and milestones in their career! A lot of our coaches are running their own successful coaching businesses or working with us on projects and coaching assignments. Most importantly our team is always around for support if a coach needs assistance closing a potential coaching opportunity or just needs mentoring and advice. Our coaches in the IL Family understand that they can come to us for support! It's an incredible feeling when I get a phone call or an email from our coaches letting me know of a new coaching assignment or project they have started and thanking us for assisting them in the progression of their career.

My story is somewhat unique…. I grew up playing basketball and ended up receiving a Division 1 scholarship and went on to eventually playing overseas in Montevideo, Uruguay and Barcelona, Spain. I eventually had a knee injury that ended my playing days at 27 years old. At this time my Dad was just relaunching his coaching business at the age of 55 and I was running my own basketball training for kids and adults. I enjoyed working with the youth and used my sports experience to mentor and help in my community. I ended up taking a full-time sales job at Lifetime Fitness. This was going to be my first experience in a different role in life, but I was up for the challenge. I was successful and ended up having the opportunity to help pre-sale a club opening up in Boston the following year! I decided to eventually go a different direction and joined a startup company called Seismic that specializes in Sales Enablement for major companies. It was a big learning curve, but I eventually got the hang of it and had a good year. That year my dad presented me with an opportunity to work with him! I was so grateful and fortunate that he wanted me to head the sales and relationships for the business! I knew when I accepted the job that I wanted to make him proud of me and I was going to do whatever it took to grow the business, sometimes waking up at 4am and staying up late to take calls from other countries. I was determined to do anything I needed to do to make sure our business was operating at a high-level.

My role now has shifted more towards building and sustaining our client and coaching relationships. I am fortunate to be able to speak with clients from all over the world, negotiating our contracts and building our relationships. What I love most about my work is the opportunities I have to travel to some of the world's most amazing places! Meeting and working with new faces, which is a true passion of mine, and I am blessed to be able to be in a human element business. Currently I am working and mentoring the millennial youth about leadership and running programs with my good friend and partner Puja Talesara! Our company is called Rewire and we are passionate about helping these young leaders become the best leaders they can be.

After joining John Mattone Global 3 years ago, my life has significantly changed. Our company now has 550 Intelligent Leadership Certified Executive Coaches that represent 53 different countries; my father John is recognized as the #1 Executive Coach in the World and we are dedicated to continuing to touch the hearts, minds and souls of everyone we encounter! We are truly here to help change the world; one leader, one coach at a time.

Nicholas Mattone

Partner & Chief Relationship Officer at John Mattone-Global, Inc.,
Millennial Leadership Coach Founder - "Rewire"

Nicholas Mattone is an expert relationship leader and a global leadership authority and Rewire Coach for millennials. Nicholas, a former Division 1 basketball player who also played professionally for four years in Uruguay and Barcelona, brings discipline, tenacity and a positive teamwork mentality to his work every day.

As Chief Relationship Officer for John Mattone-Global, Nicholas is responsible for building and sustaining strong relationships with a global network of clients, prospects, partners, coaches, franchisees, and the media. Nicholas is the "glue" that brings the JMG internal and external teams together and keeps them together in support of the JMG vision, mission and purpose. While Nicholas is out of the office he enjoys going to the gym, playing basketball, and relaxing with his friends and family.

nick@johnmattone.com

https://johnmattone.com/

https://www.linkedin.com/in/nicholas-mattone-982688110/

13

Finding Your Unique Formula: the Wisdom Within the Coach

BY MAXX ANGENETTA JONES

My name is Maxx and I am a professional life and relationship coach. I help clients develop a greater understanding of themselves, family dynamics, work relationships, personal relationships with others, and to gain a deeper understanding of their spiritual world. It is critical that clients understand and appreciate who they are, what their purpose is and how to create a positive future for themselves.

I have been engaged in this endeavor for a long time and I want to provide something that would take the pressure off coaches and coaching. I want to work on having professionals focus their energy on their coaching, and on tasks they excel in.

My idea is to help my fellow coaches and those new to the business, so I created Life Coaching Today. This a platform where you, as a professional can post your biography. , your blog, and even your videos. Any and all ways a client can find you is included so they can learn what you have to offer. It allows the client to give you a review once they have approved of your services. Life Coaching Today is connected to

Google, Siri, Katana and all other major search engines across the world. And it works!

Whenever I think back to my beginnings, I realize how important these supports have been. With guidance and a network of support, mistakes would be minimal. I have discussed this with other coaches, and we are very consistent in our thinking.

My motivation for becoming a life coach was the desire to help people improve their lives.

A few months ago, we launched a new magazine entitled Life Coaching Today. We wanted to create an opportunity where we could feature coaches who are trying to build a career of their own, and giving them some exposure to prospective clients who may have a need for additional support in their lives.

My goal for this platform is to turn coaching into something similar to counselling or going to a mental health therapist. Creating awareness and providing options that offer support is the fundamental objective.

In the next few paragraphs I will identify various ideas that will help improve training of new coaches. The ultimate goal is continual improvement.

I started life coaching long before I received my first certification. I felt the need to help people with their personal growth, to help them better understand their choices – be it positive and negative. It really is that simple. There are always things people do not know about themselves; the good they do but also the possible harm or damage they may cause. Even if it was unintentional, it still happened, and healing is needed. So, with some very hit and miss experiences behind me, I hit the ground running.

Yet, every day I think back, and I wish there was a moment I could point to and say, 'There! That is what made me want to do this!'

As a new coach I identified my number one goal: How do I get clients? I had already determined my niche; I had already determined how I wanted to help people and why. Now I just had to get those people in the door!

Perseverance is definitely key. When all this started, I learnt an important first lesson - that if it doesn't work try again and again and again until you figure out what does. This is the grueling part of a job that is known as earning your stripes! We have all done it and it's a major part of the reason we are still in business.

Of all the professional coaches I have met in my time, those that worry me most are the business coaches. I've seen a lot of coaches fail along the way and there was a lot of heartache as people's hopes and dreams crumbled. They put their faith in the wrong things.

There are so many business coaches out there offering all sorts of enticements but no actual evidence of growth or progress. They point to money as the only motivating factor but what we do is different. Our job is to help clients grow and appreciate their lives. That is our motivation.

I chose to focus on my coaching and nothing else, but I also wanted to gain as much raw experience as I possibly could. Because it was the work that mattered, I chose to charge only a small amount for my coaching. For me it was about the people involved, it was never about the money. I judge my success by my clients' successes. My achievements were passed by word of mouth. Even today it's still an amazing thing to know a happy client's whole demeanor is advertising my services! I firmly believe you need to give the best you have to your clients both in and out the office or why bother do this job at all?

A person's growth GPS can't tell time, after all.

But let's get back to the matter at hand, my calling and perhaps, yours?

I can't say this enough but if you want to help people; you should be involved with those people. Let them bring their lives to you! If nothing else, it gives their problems some background. Life coaching is a hands-on experience; it has to be that way and the more knowledge you have the better you will be able to do your job. You have to want to communicate to your clients and make your presence known in a meaningful way. Show your clients who you are.

Here is my list of seven things I would like you to understand in order to develop your career.

1. Stay away from unscrupulous business coaches. You will not make money and may even lose money.

2. Utilize social media to market yourself. Identify as many social media sites as you can and get involved.

3. Let Google help and teach you. Google has teaching videos on many subjects but some of the best are about how to use Google to help you and your businesses.

   Interview other coaches. Get to know your colleagues and develop networking skills.

4. Invite other coaches to post on your site. It's another great way of networking and an opportunity to learn from other coaches - veterans and novices alike.

   I have always preferred to be face-to-face with my clients, posting videos and thought-provoking questions excites and triggers interest and curiosity. Reading answers from a diverse group of people is fascinating.

5. Whatever part of our mutual craft you choose to specialise in, take public speaking classes. Speaking clearly is necessary to be a successful coach. When you finish those classes put them to good use. Get in front of potential clients and talk to them about something interesting and insightful.

I've said it before, and I will say it again: Our business is people. Get to know them and try to understand them. Taking an interest is the simplest way to get people to take an interest in you.

6. Everything requires practice, so make every minute of every day useful in one form or another. Like brainstorming with your client and finding a solution to their dilemma. Study or even doing chores, make it work for you.

7. Try not to rush. Instead think things through and develop patience. Build the components of your business slowly so they will last.

I believe that to be a good coach, a successful coach, you must let your clients see what you have to offer. By following the steps above I can guarantee you will be successful in finding your clients and becoming the good they desire to see in this world.

I am also building a Coaching Conference - this event will facilitate ways new coaches can meet and talk with coaches that have more experience. It is crucial that we pick those who are beneficial to you. People who can answer your questions, and can explain what needs to be done and more importantly, why? By attending this conference opportunities to meet potential clients abound.

Also, be aware of unscrupulous business coaches who exploit those clients that are emotionally vulnerable offering vague or unrealistic promises. They manipulate others for their own personal gain.

Our goal as mentioned earlier is to help people, not take advantage of them at a time of distress.

At the end of the day, it's all about focusing on your coaching style, growing it, refining it. Each step, each class you take, each piece of advice from those wiser than you leads to building a professional attitude. Life coaches need to be respectful in all of their interactions. Respect is the basis for developing trust and confidence. Life coaching is really about the relationship one has with their clients.

To be the best you can be for your clients is your goal, so no matter where you are someone will find you on Life Coaching Today's platform or read about you in the magazine and decide, 'Yes that's the one for me.'

Maxx Angenetta Jones

Master Certified Relationship Coach, Master Hypnotist, NLP Master Practitioner,

Following my education, I decided to pursue a career in Life Coaching. Working with individuals in need of guidance in their lives appealed to me. My desire to help people better focus on developing healthy relationships and offer ideas to improve personal growth and of course, offer support, advice and understanding as they work to improve and strengthen family ties has been a very challenging and rewarding experience.

My coaching career began by attending the Certified Life Coaching Institute where I achieved my Master Coaching Certification. I wanted to go deeper and from there I attended Sedona Metaphysical University. At that point, I decided to become a certified NLP practitioner and finally to become a Master Hypnotist at the Banyan Hypnosis Centre.

By immersing myself in the latest theories and treatments, I had the opportunity to study healing in a whole new way. All of the advances and various techniques were laid out before me and my thirst for learning continued unabated.

Over time my coaching focus evolved. My interest now includes having my clients focus on current relationships and developing a better understanding of themselves, emphasizing an analysis of "Self "in their home and business lives. Using my experience, skill set and knowledge to help people explore and achieve to their full potential is my ultimate goal. To that end, I have started Life Coaching Today in order to help other coaches and clients find each other.

Facebook – maxx.jones

14

Daddy, what's a "Leader"?

BY MARK LAITFLANG STONE

"Daddy, what's a Leader?" After an awkward silence that lasted a good minute and a half, I realized two of Life's great lessons. One - if you can't convey an idea to a child, you really shouldn't be preaching to the choir. Two - Leadership is a Choice.

Try explaining the idea of leadership to a six-year-old. The weight of each word hangs in the air, as your child looks at you in reverent silence and anticipation. For a moment that seems like an eternity, the fate of the world rests in your hands as you attempt to pass on the wisdom of the ages to your progeny. There she is, your legacy. And every lesson you've learnt about life, love and failure rushes forth for recognition as you ramble on like a madman.

Oh, the agony!

We throw the word Leader around so often, we've trivialized the word, slapping on addendums and adjectives like "bossy", "capitalist" and "tyrant", with definitions as diverse as "follower", "Gandhian" and "fall guy". But on a Sunday afternoon as the monsoon set her sights on our city, I realized more about leadership than serial entrepreneurship has ever taught me.

If you've built teams and broken ground with sheer persistence, you'll know that our greatest personal challenge as coaches aren't the words we speak. It is the actions we consistently take that set an example for our children and the people who trust us to lead. Whether you like it or not, this truth in particular is hard to escape. You stop being a coach when you're home.

Your home is your safe space. Your private corner of freedom where your actions don't necessarily have to align with your last great leadership rant. You'd be lying if you said you practice what you preach. If you aren't, I'm pleasantly surprised!

Something I read a long time ago rings true today- "Talk is cheap!" Across audiences and workshops over the last sixteen years, the question that has stayed with me is - "Whose list is my name on?".

This list is a great place to start with if, like me, your mission is to permanently impact the lives of the people you coach and work with. You'll need a pen and a piece of paper to answer these questions for yourself.

Quieten your mind, sit back and think about this for a while.

Who are the people who have had the most significant impact on your life?

You have exactly thirty seconds to write out your list.

My children are my safe space. My daughter is all of ten now and my son is busy dancing his way into the next decade at five, as I watch the afternoon sun streak across golden-green blades of grass in the fields beyond our guest house.

Their names are on my list.

Next, I'd like you to describe the impact each person has had on your life. Since we aren't doing this together, I promise you this will work best if you choose one powerful quality that sums up the person. Write that down next to their names.

By this point, I'd imagine the word "impact" doesn't mean what it meant two minutes ago. I have ten people on my list. Here's a few to begin with:

- Maisha taught me what **responsibility** means. My daughter's birth made me want to be a better man.
- Badonbor forced me to come to terms with who I wanted to be as a father. My son teaches me **truth**, every day.
- My father, Vincent, demonstrated **kindness** and **love** in all that he did. He was the bravest man I knew in the face of adversity and brokenness. I wanted to be just like him when I grew up.
- My grade 10 teacher, a Christian missionary, taught me the power of **encouragement**. If it wasn't for his belief in me, public speaking would have died a natural death early on in my life.
- Through her death, my mother-in-law, Durga, proved beyond a shadow of a doubt that impact, can be **quiet** and **serene**, etched with love into our lives.
- My wife, Aishisha has become the voice of reason over the course of 16 years of partnership. Through good old-fashioned common sense and unconditional love, she has shown me the path to **consistency**.
- My mother, Cecelia moved mountains to keep our family fed through the years when my father could not. Her indominable spirit showed us what grit was made of. She didn't know it then, but I'll say it now. My mother taught me **courage**.

Great Leadership makes you **want** to be a better human being.

I don't know about you, but my list of thirty seconds is filled with the names of people who made me want to change. They did this not by the words they spoke, but by the way they made me **feel**. They coached me to be a better person through the examples they set and the standards they demanded of me, for me.

It shouldn't surprise you then, that I have yet to name a coach on my list.

How many people do you think would put **your** name down on their lists?

What then, is the true measure of your personal impact?

Whose list are you on?

I challenge you to write down as many names as you can in the next two minutes. You may also choose to write down- in a single word or a brief phrase, your impact in their lives.

If you're having trouble finding names, you're not alone. Eight out of ten participants average two names on this list. The number doesn't get better as you grow older. I've had a fifty-five-year-old coach confess that she couldn't place a single name on her list.

If you can't find a name to place on your list, it's because you've forgotten that coaching begins in your safe space. The impact that coaching-by-example has on the people you love, is powerful.

Everyone, then, is a coach. And everyone has a story of impact waiting to be written.

As parents, we must begin by acknowledging that leadership starts at home. In the choices we make, and the quality of our interactions and interpersonal spaces. Almost everything said, seen and unseen is constantly under the watchful eyes of our children, being absorbed and imbibed when we least realize it.

At Home, as in Life, we must lead with Love.

As teachers, we are the bridge between a generation's absence of purpose, and our children's conviction in change. Classrooms are in many ways our last bastions of hope, as we come to terms with a world that is quickly running out of breath as we engage in irresponsible demands on our environment and our communities. Today's conflicts question our humanity. In schools and colleges across the planet, leadership must be enshrined in our teaching pedagogies, equipping children to confront an uncertain future with integrity and tolerance.

At School, as in Life, we must lead with Purpose.

As employees and employers, we constantly articulate our values and beliefs through our business practices and the dignity we attach to labour. Every sacrifice made. Every policy adopted. Every challenge surmounted. Each action taken when accountable, transparent and responsible is an inspiration to the participant's industry. These benchmarks are intangible, but worth far more than the assets on our balance sheets. These benchmarks can transform a business from a brand, to a trademark. And for a select few who craft a special connection with consumers, trademarks can become what an inspirational global branding guru calls "Lovemarks".

At Work, as in Life, we must lead by Example. Responsibly.

As leaders elected to power, the battle of choice is a tour-de-force that either serves a greater good, or a lesser evil. Are we the agents of change our children would be proud of? At what cost is our common minimum mandate achieved? In a world that lays claim to being more connected and aware than at any other time in our collective history, the disparity in equality in even the most basic fundamental rights enshrined in our constitutions, are an everyday reality for millions. How does a child from the rural Khasi, Garo or Jaintia Hills in my corner of the world – Meghalaya in North East India, cross the massive divide in education, culture and opportunity with dignity and self-worth?

In Politics, as in Life, we must lead for the Greater Good.

As coaches blazing a trail in our areas of expertise, we cannot forget that we are responsible for the well-being, resilience and aspiration of our clients and the organisations we work with. In my corner of the world, life coaching has a real shot at transforming and adding value to formal education frameworks as we work towards preparing tribal youth for the challenges of life and careers. Our programmes are framed around an approach that integrates mindset coaching, emotional awareness, human connection and communication with incremental actions that help young people take charge of their lives. In doing so, my tribe of coaches has worked with over 50,000 people in North East India.

In small communities where life-coaching is making its first appearance, the examples set by senior coaches on the circuit through their choices and actions outside of the actual coaching experience, are paramount to sustaining impact.

In Coaching, as in Life, we must lead with Consistency.

In each of our roles- coaches, parents, teachers, executives, entrepreneurs, employees, politicians or the clergy, the question of Leadership leaves much to be answered. Throughout history though, the themes of Love, Purpose, Example and Responsibility have stood the test of time. Now more than ever, Leadership is less about titles and authority and more about making inspiring choices.

The poet and writer, Kahlil Gibran's verses connect our souls with a wisdom that is timeless. One of my favourite passages speaks of leadership, children and choices: "Yes, there is a Nirvana; it is in leading your sheep to a green pasture, and in putting your child to sleep, and in writing the last line of your poem."

What will be the last line of your poem? Our stories are written in gold through the consistent actions and quiet promises we make to ourselves when we think no one's looking.

As coaches, our impact begins when we leave our pedagogies, paradigm shifts and protocols at the door and choose to focus on the story we are writing with the people we love.

Pulling up under a Jacaranda tree in all its purple glory, I turned off the engine, and allowed the evening sun to settle on the twinkle in her eye. Leadership, to my six year old - Maisha, and a conversation that shall forever remind me of the complexity of Choice.

--

Maisha: "Well?"

Me: "Well what, Maisha?"

Maisha: "What's a Leader Daddy?"

Me: "A Leader is a Who, Maisha. Not a What!"

Maisha: "Who's a Leader Daddy?"

Me: "A leader is a good person. Someone that other people want to listen to and follow!"

Maisha: "Is a Boss a Leader?"

Me: "Yes. But not all bosses are good people."

Maisha: "What is a good person?"

Me: "A person who makes really good choices! And tries her best not to make bad choices."

Maisha: "Daddy."

Me: "Yes?"

Maisha: "How do you know when something is good or bad? Who taught you that?"

--

Truth be told, that last question would have surprised anyone.

It's often said that we are the result of our choices. Our children are this generation's next great frontier and the choices we make shall define the quality of leadership we leave behind.

As we head into the future and question everything that was once a constant, we are left to answer humanity's bravest question.

You know what it is.

"Who taught you that?"

Mark Laitflang Stone

Social Entrepreneur, Coach, Speaker,
Founder Avenues, North East India & Pockets of Happiness

Mark Laitflang Stone is a pioneering Social Entrepreneur whose coaching framework for personal growth and well-being has impacted over 50,000 lives in India's North-Eastern region. His inspiring journey began in his home in the clouds, Shillong, a hillstation nestled in the foothills of the Himalayas, now home to his flourishing coaching organisation, Avenues. From dropping out of high school and selling flowers at 16 to coaching audiences in India, Europe and South East Asia through human experiences that he calls "Pockets of Happiness", Mark's own story of courage and resilience is deeply moving.

Over the course of the last sixteen years, he has emerged as his region's leading authority in life coaching interventions for youth and leadership development for executives and entrepreneurs. His unique philosophy unlocks Confidence, Clarity and Purpose for everyone and takes forward his personal mission to help people own their stories and embrace their impact in an uncertain world. Avenues' flagship programmes are working towards augmenting formal education structures with life coaching efforts, significantly improving the quality of life and careers for tribal youth. When he isn't running his teams, Mark can be found at one of his many speaking engagements inspiring audiences to rediscover their values and deliver their "message to the world" to an unsuspecting camera. Mark lives in Shillong, the picturesque capital of the state of Meghalaya, India with his wife and children.

LinkedIn Profile https://www.linkedin.com/in/marklstone/
Facebook & Instagram Handle @markstoneinspires
Twitter Handle @mark_inspires
www.markstoneinspires.com

15

10 Common Mistakes Coaches Make

BY DIVYA LV JEGASUNDARAM

"Somewhere along the way, we must learn that there is nothing greater than to do something for others." –Martin Luther King, Jr.

Ask most coaches why they decided to become a coach, and you will often hear that it was because they felt that it was part of their life purpose. A calling. A way to give back. To help others. Sometimes, this feeling is coupled with something in their career that has gone wrong, or that moment of feeling unfulfilled or that 'is this all there is to my life?' moment.

As coaches, I believe we are in a uniquely wonderful position of being able to help and serve in a way that is impactful, personal and tailored to each individual's goals, desires or aspirations. We get to be that cheer leader, friend, pillar of support and confidante while also being able to challenge, question, play devil's advocate and stretch the minds of our clients in a way that will never be perceived as confrontational or bossy…if you do it right!

I believe that it is this helpful, selfless, giving part of being a coach that appeals to most clients and that this is why many enjoy and value the time they have in their sessions; because it's that undivided attention that a person gets to have with someone focusing entirely on them, their life, their goals and their challenges. At no point in their coaching session are they expected to be considerate in their conversation. A client is entitled to be self-centered in their session because this is their time, they set the agenda, explore their thoughts, take time to strategize how to overcome their challenges and obstacles, eliminate their fears and anything else they want to address.

For the past 7 years, I have been fortunate enough to not only be a full time coach but also a senior lecturer within a very esteemed international coaching school. My time in this role has given me great insights into the minds of new, aspiring and seasoned coaches, seeing them from being wide eyed students to certified coaches. Therefore, in this chapter I would like to, from my experience, address 10 common mistakes I see coaches make.

1. Never Experiencing a Coaching Session

I'm continually shocked when I ask a coach if they have ever experienced coaching, and the response is a 'no.' I then follow up with, 'if you've never invested in yourself, why would you expect your clients to?' To which, I'm usually confronted with…silence. I have found that those who have experienced coaching, however basic or advance, will most certainly have a better understanding of what coaching entails, how it works, the benefits, the purpose, the advantages of working with a coach etc.

This seems like a trivial point, but those coaches who have never experienced coaching, or have never spent time, money or energy into investing in themselves, do in fact struggle to believe that others would invest in the same. They have more doubts as to whether coaching and the process works, and they question their own value in the process.

2. Believing That the Coaching Market Is Scarce

A common fear I have witnessed with new and established coaches is that the market for coaches is scarce. For a new coach it's whether there will be enough business for them, and for the established ones, it's whether the pool of potential clients is going to diminish, given that the industry is growing so rapidly, and new coaches are coming in and often charging less. In my opinion, this fear is unfounded. I believe that no matter how many people take an interest in coaching, or how many established coaches already exist, there is most certainly enough business for all those who want it. Instead, it's this limiting belief that ends up creating fear in coaches which often results in the creation of excuses, which then results in often giving up before they've started. I can safely say that to adopt a mindset of abundance rather than scarcity will serve you better here.

3.   Understand Your Role as a Coach

For every coach, their relationship with each of their clients will be unique, and unless your client has already experienced coaching, then for many, this can start off as a pretty daunting experience, whether it be mixed emotions, uncertainty of reaching the goal itself, the cost of coaching and what the overall value will be. It is important to remember that the very act of even approaching or hiring you, a coach, will have been thought about and the idea tossed around for a while, along with attempting to achieve their goals without you. Therefore when you are the coach of choice, take your role in your client's life seriously.

Take time to get to know your client and their goal so that you understand what your role in their life will be, and if you choose to be their coach, then take it as a responsibility. Show up. Listen. Encourage and believe. Challenge and question. Motivate and inspire. Be attentive and care…for it is you that they chose.

Personally, I consider my relationship with my clients to be a sacred one. As their coach, I take a position in their lives where their trust, dreams and aspirations are shared, along with their biggest challenges, obstacles and fears. I become their confidante, sounding board and sometimes the most trusted person in their lives. It is truly an honor and privilege to be this person, so remembering that and striving to give your best in every session will make your relationship a truly beautiful one.

4.   Speaking Vs Coaching

There is scope for you to be a coach as well as have opportunities to speak. In fact, many would agree that part of being a coach, whether you like it or not is also to speak. Through speaking we get to do something that in regular coaching sessions is forbidden. We get to speak about our own experiences, lessons learnt, failure, success or anything else for that matter. As a speaker you are given an opportunity to motivate and inspire your audience through stories of your life. For many coaches, speaking will also give prospects some insight into who you are, what you've done and most importantly how you can help them achieve their goals and dreams. So what is the common mistake I refer to here? Often I hear people tell me they want to be coaches because they love to talk, or because they have been through so much or have done so much in their lives that they can help advise and tell others on what needs to be done. Loving speaking and advising doesn't mean that coaching is necessarily the right fit for you. Likewise if you really want to coach, but hate speaking it doesn't mean that you can't be a good coach either.

Quite simply, take some time to understand firstly where your interests lie, and secondly which comes more naturally to you. What are you own goals and aspirations? What is your own vision and mission as a coach? Once you know this, you can decide accordingly how to go about incorporating this into your coach identity.

5.   Time Management

Do not underestimate the level of time management that is involved with ensuring your coaching business runs smoothly and efficiently. For many, starting their coaching business means going from an employee to an entrepreneur, and while it seems great at the beginning because you feel you're free and you get to manage yourself and not be answerable to anyone, this will soon wear off. Scheduling the right number of appointments in a day, setting a daily 'hours of operation' schedule with breaks etc will also help you in managing your time effectively. One of the biggest problems that will arise from you not effectively managing your time will be that your clients suffer because the time and attention you give them consciously or unconsciously will be divided.

6. Personal Development

As William S. Burroughs said, 'If you're not growing, you're dying.' The personal development journey for all of us is a never ending one. It's a process that we can never get enough of, or that we already have enough of. As coaches, it's imperative that you consistently plan time for our own development. Obtaining your certification isn't enough to carry you through your entire career as coach. As much as coaches look forward to clients hiring them for achieving goals and overcoming challenges, there is almost always a part of coaches that is also wanting to embark upon a personal development journey for themselves. Therefore if you, as a coach, have no further interest or desire to better yourself or develop your mind, then you will likely find yourself only being able to help your client to a certain point where your role as a coach is restricted.

Personal development can happen through reading, taking courses, attending seminars, gaining further certifications or working with your own coach to work on your development. For many of us, the desire to keep growing is there and we think we will get to it; remember - we help our clients with this very step and then neglect our own growth! So why not take a moment right now, to make a note of 3 things that you want to work on that will help you grow as a human being, personally or professionally, followed by making a commitment to make this happen.

7. Coaching Isn't Just 1:1

Who said coaching can only be 1:1? As you will have all learnt by now, coaching can be done in many ways, other than working with a client 1 to 1. When you can start opening up your mind to multiple ways of working with your client and thinking outside of that ever so rigid box we like to sit so comfortably in, then you will find the possibilities are endless here. Whether it be group coaching online or in person, courses, workshops, teleseminars or retreats, remember you have the freedom to create. So, get creative. You don't need to follow traditional coaching methods to create impactful sessions, nor do you have to limit yourself to thinking that you physically have to conduct the sessions.

8.   Not Valuing The Certification Process

Please…Please…Please…Coaches…VALUE   YOUR CREDENTIALS!!! Value the investment you made in yourself, whether it be through time, energy or money. To get certified, maybe you made certain sacrifices, so don't downplay this when you are either talking to other coaches or prospective clients. Even if you are someone who has been coaching for years before your certification, or informally, something drove you to get certified and give what you were doing some extra meaning. Agreed, there are many courses available nowadays that may vary in price, duration, in person or distance learning. Whichever path you have chosen for yourself carries its own value because it has required you to start with the fundamentals and basics followed by finding a niche and honing your skills. Understand that if you don't value yourself and the work you do then you can't expect your clients to. You must adopt a confidence and belief within you that you are the very best person to help your clients achieve their goals.

9.   Journaling the "WINS."

Journaling is an increasingly popular concept that I hear many coaches suggest to their clients during sessions. Yet again, not something that I see too many coaches do for themselves. Journaling doesn't have to be a laborious task that you struggle to schedule time to complete. To journal is to simply make a note. Therefore, any which way you like to make notes, do that. As for journaling the 'WINS', my reason for this is to simply be able to have a tool to remind yourself of your wins as a coach, particularly on those down days, or days that you feel maybe your session wasn't as impactful, or when you're wondering why you left your six - figure salary, your safe predictable job, or your career that you hated but made money in. Reading back your WINS will absolutely remind you of your 'why – your purpose', followed by reinforcing your path and efforts as well as reenergizing you to stay motivated and to keep going.

10. Being Scared or Reluctant to Share Knowledge

This last one always leaves me a little stumped, which is the very reason I chose the opening quote by Martin Luther King Jr at the beginning of this chapter. If you have ever helped a person in your life you will know, understand and most likely remember even just a snippet of how you felt. Helping, sharing, supporting - one of the main purposes of this book you have in your hands today, and so why have I included this as a common mistake coaches make? It's here on this list because it's shocking how only a few people are actually willing to share their journey, what worked for them, what didn't work, what were the failures, what are the sure ways to succeed, what were the fears, what was some of the self talk, what was it like to put your heart and soul into a proposal and then get rejected, what was it like to write your first blog and not have anyone like or appreciate it.

These are just a few of the experiences one faces being on this journey and while even the most experienced or successful coaches have lived this, very few will talk of it, let alone share their lessons learnt, and the ones that do will often still withhold information for fear of 'over sharing' or 'giving away too much.' With the coaching industry evolving and coaches genuinely seeking guidance and mentorship, please share your knowledge, be a mentor, be a guide and take pride in the giving of this help.

The above are just 10 of the most common challenges that I have seen occurring time after time as coaches embark upon their journey. Granted, not all of these will be applicable to you, but it is my belief that if you can visit these points and evaluate for yourself where you are in your journey then you will be able to easily pinpoint your developmental areas. As coaches, we have a duty to the clients we serve and ourselves to keep growing, learning and striving for excellence.

Divya LV Jegasundaram

Certified Fulfillment Life & Business Coach, Keynote, International Speaker, 2x Best-Selling Author, Creator of Coach Wisdom & Nominee of Canada's Top 40 Under 40 2019

Divya LV Jegasundaram is a 2-time best-selling author, certified fulfillment life coach, mentor, senior lecturer, keynote speaker and proud creator of Coach Wisdom. Divya spent more than 13 years as a successful banker before gaining her certification as Coach in 2013.

Internationally known for her work, Divya is recognized and honored for her career success and service to society. Focus, ambition and a strong personal drive have been inherent qualities that Divya has emulated in all aspects of her social, family and professional life.

Different life experiences piqued her interest and passion for helping others to formulate, shape and achieve their goals, dreams and desires, which is how she became the youngest bank manager in both the UK and North America. Her ability to affect others positively is born from a patient and understanding temperament, a strong will, extraordinary drive and a humanity that radiates and embraces those around her.

Divya's ongoing efforts helped her quickly be recognized as a young woman with an ability to motivate, inspire and empower those she meets and works with. Her enthusiasm in sharing the profession and benefits of coaching with the masses, has resulted in her being able to deeply impact and empower her clients to lead and live a fulfilled life.

Divya was also an Award Winner of the WIM Canada (Women in Management) Upcoming Entrepreneur Award, the Woman On Fire Business Woman of the Year Award and in 2019, nominated as one of Canada's Top 40 Under 40.

IG @divyacoachlife

www.coachlifeplaylife.com

16

Coaching is poetry in motion

BY NASREEN VARIYAWA

"I rock my role as Author Coach because I am the champion of originality.
I never do anything just ordinary and that's what I brand Nasreeniology.
Come on, read on, let me influence your Coaching if you dare
Let Nasreeniology fill the blanks that will otherwise be left bare."

1.   Can I, Should I, or Must I?

If you have often asked yourself whether you can, should or must go into coaching, then you probably have had a feeling somewhere inside of you that this is something you could probably excel at.

Whether you can or can't is something you alone know. What I know for sure is that if you have ever coached someone at work, at home, on the sports ground or over a cup of coffee, then you have innate potential that you should exploit. I am by no means implying that you do not need to be a certified coach, but I would like you to imagine what a power-house you could be if you pursued both your qualification and your innate talents. The bottom line here is that everyone needs to start somewhere. So, here's an initial thought for you to begin with:

"You may never be able to change the world, but you can make a start You'll create some sparks in some minds, one by one from your heart."

2. The 'Itch' that Must be 'Scratched'

Once you have stopped sitting on the fence (a rather painful place to be) and have established your niched coaching business, it is normal to wonder how you will convert potential clients into paying ones. I am not talking about only promoting your brand here. As far as I am concerned, YOU are your brand and people buy into you before they buy into what you have to offer. When I first started out, I did a lot of pro bono work to establish my name and reputation. When people found out who the force behind some best- selling books was, they voluntarily hired me.

So, the first thing to do is to set up a FREE coaching call with your prospective clients. What you say, how you say it and how you make them feel is crucial to hooking and keeping your client. The world of social media offers some opportunities to get to know potential clients. What you want to do is put together a basic strategy for hooking your client. When they talk to me about their book ideas, I can already deduce where their books are headed and am able to help them gain clarity on the vision for their books quickly. I facilitate them to a stage in the process I call 'The Itch.' What this means is that I get them so excited with the clarity they receive that they are itching to get off the call with me and get straight to writing their books (with me as their coach of course). To give your clients an 'Itch' that needs to be 'scratched' you need to always:

"Plan before you speak and inspire meaningful action Plan before you speak and aim for more than satisfaction."

3. Ding Dong! Anybody home?

Negotiating and establishing a plan of action at the outset is probably one of the most important things you can do. I use a simple project plan that I share with my clients to map the details of writing their books, the number of chapters, the content, the deadlines and the final steps to finishing up their projects. Very often prospective authors come to me with ideas and talent but no real aptitude to approach the book. This is when I have 'Ding Dong! Anybody home?' moments to deal with. When my clients and I mutually put their project plans together, the lightbulbs are switched on and they rush off to write their books. The takeaway here is to always provide something tangible for clients to work with because quick, visible results are money spinners.

"Planning is the key, a roadmap set in motion Goals set in detail, reap rewards like a magic potion"

4.   Smoke it Like a Larnie and Chat to Guru Gut

When I taught listening skills, I often taught the difference between listening and hearing and used the analogy of smoking cigarettes. In South Africa, poor people often smoke the leftovers (stompies) cast aside by other more affluent family members and friends, referred to as larnies. What I taught is that hearing is like *smoking stompies* (you don't really get to enjoy the pleasure that comes with smoking a full cigarette) whereas listening is like *smoking it like a larnie* (you have all the time to enjoy a full cigarette). I always encouraged my audience to *smoke it like a larnie* (shame on me). I shamelessly use the same strategy in my coaching business because I believe that before I can give my clients 'The Itch', I need to be able to tap into my intuition. I have named my intuition *Guru Gut* and tap into it after *I have smoked it like a larnie*. This is the crux of coaching for me and I find myself connecting with clients in ways that are unsuspecting. You see, as coaches we tend to focus a lot more on the academia and a lot less on the people we are coaching. A one size fits all approach does not work in coaching. Each client is unique and to win them over you must be able to tap into what they are NOT saying and then give them the courage to write exactly that. Why? Because this is what sells a book. Therefore,

"Listen! Listen between the lines, listen so you know, exactly what's on the mind Guru gut is your trusted friend, don't switch off the voice within Let Guru Gut work his magic on you, there is more value in this than you think."

5. Imagination is True Intelligence

I can hear you scoffing right now but this is my story and I'm sticking to it. I have always used a combination of knowledge and imagination to do most of the things I have accomplished in life, including coaching authors. My vision for whatever I do has always begun with the end in mind. Successfully coaching someone requires that you pay attention to what clients envision and use it on two levels. The first is to plan for them to write books that are in line with their vision. The second is to get them to express what they envision for themselves at a book launch, a conference at which they are invited to speak, a cover for the book, a blurb, a book signing or a networking event for authors. I have found that the latter gives clients more of 'The Itch' than any other kind of motivation. Asking leading questions about what their success looks like in their imaginations tells them that you are interested in getting them to succeed. To do this, you may need to change your own way of doing things, like beginning with the end in mind:

"Listen up, let me tell you something wise - open up your heart and tap into your mind; Find the eye there that's exists deep within; when you tap into it you'll discover your imagination"

6. By Hook or By Brook

In this rapidly growing market of coaches, the only way to survive is to be authentic. Your clients must be respected and honored rather than be treated like fools. Being authentic means that you must be sincere, honest, dedicated, committed, explicitly trusted and yes, very original. Clients that come to you with their stories, memoirs, autobiographies and business secrets are all putting their lives into your hands. Whilst you cannot guarantee that every authors book can be a best seller, you must demonstrate that you will do whatever it takes to give their books due attention. Treat every client alike. Be fair and be helpful, even after their books have been published. This is what will bring you repeat business. It will also ensure referrals. Ninety percent of my clients have been referred to me by past or existing clients because I chose to hook them rather than crook them. So, remember:

"Trust, honesty and integrity, should be your qualities innate, it's YOU they buy into, so stand out, don't hesitate People will remember you, not so much for what you do, but the impression you leave on them and the perception they have of you"

7. Soar or Saw

To give your clients the best, you must be at your best. It's as simple as that. As a coach, soaring means that you will have to develop yourself all the time. Talking to others in the business, exchanging simple experiences, reading books, taking online courses, attending conferences, giving workshops, watching videos or using any other intervention that helps you to grow. Experiential learning is wonderful if you can accept developmental criticism. Get a coach if you don't have one. I have asked my coach to let me watch him in action and I have let my coach watch me in action. There is truly nothing to be afraid of if you approach your vocation in the spirit of continuous learning. In short, choose to *soar* at your vocation rather than *saw* it to death. You ought to:

"Review what you have been told, to see if there is any weight And if there's a chance you could be better, then learn the lessons in haste"

8. Coaching is Poetry in Motion

I believe in the power of one and what this means is that it takes just one of something to make a change. Whether that's just a sentence or an idea or someone who believes in your vision, the world makes magnificent strides towards positive change through the power of one. As a coach, you have the power of one right there in your head, heart and soul and you ought not to forget it or take it lightly.

"If coaching is your vocation, you have chosen poetry in motion Your role is magnanimous, not small by any notion Every time you elevate, motivate or share ideas Nations grow with more people who aspire to inspire."

Nasreen Variyawa

Author Coach, Author of 3 Amazon Best-Sellers, Editor & Ghost Writer.

Born and raised in Durban, South Africa, Author Coach Nasreen Variyawa has 3 Amazon.com best-sellers to her credit. An editor and ghost-author too, she is the creative force behind many other best-sellers. She has written a few articles for online news agencies and is known for her unique take on various topics, including Leadership lessons you will learn at any Indian wedding and Leadership Principles for Divorce. Her niche is helping other unknown aspiring authors to achieve the dream of becoming published in as short a time span as possible. She enjoys working with first time authors from diverse backgrounds and specializes in helping them realize their vision, their strategy and finally their book. A post-graduate in education leadership and management, Nasreen has also inspired, motivated and elevated thousands of corporate learners through workshops she has conducted over the years and specializes in using simple poetry to inspire, motivate, elevate and influence her audience. She published a collection of these poems in Aspire to Inspire: Poems that elevate your speech. She believes strongly in the Power of One and to this end has written, "One thought, one vision, one dream, one sentence, one willing student and one willing cheerleader can change your entire world. Whether you are the student or the cheerleader, both worlds change for the better."

Her forthcoming work includes a book tentatively titled, Apple Fetish for Authors- simple recipes for a fabulous authoring career.

www.nasreeniology.com
www.facebook.com/authornasreenv
www.linkedin/in/nasreenv
www.amazon.com/author/nasreenvariyawa

17

The Principle of Auto-Coaching

BY DEXTER J RODRIGUES

"*The art of giving begins with the art of receiving*" said my first Life Coach. I remember completing eight coaching sessions with him and over the years, this one line has found its way foremost into my golden principles of living a purposeful life.

What does it hold for you dear reader?

Imagine as a coach, to be able to refine your skills or self-educate on your coaching style while the coaching conversation is still on; filling your 'a-ha' toolbox, not **post** but **during** your discussion with the client. All this, while you help unravel for the client; a dialogue of discovery fueled by your mindset of genuine service fulfilment. This self-tutoring exercise leads you to gleaning or *receiving* valuable life and coaching lessons while providing for or *giving* your client unconstrained support. The resulting Eureka moment is not just for your client but for you too and therein lies the intrinsic fun of it.

Auto-coaching, which knits several elements together, as one might suspect, is neither the privilege of chess grandmasters who calculate several steps ahead, nor is it limited to only coaches.

The benefits of instant introspection and subsequent steering can and should be employed by just about anyone willing to sharpen their proverbial saw.

You may ask - How can one, while facilitating discussion, remain in continuous cognizance of *how* one is conducting the coaching conversation. How do you step out of the transaction while still in it and observe, evaluate and keep directing and re-directing the meandering flow of thought and word.

The trick in captaining the game is by becoming both, a spectator to and player of the sport.

What are the tools required? What is the mindset required? And what is the deeper sense of purpose that this principle postulates, not just for coaches but for the self-leader?

"Do what you love in the service of people who love what you do" wrote Steve Farber in the management classic 'The Radical Leap'.

Let's begin this leap just as how we begin all our coaching conversations; with Exploration.

Being Truly Alive and Pre-conditioning

There is a fascinating tale of a 16th century emperor who went by the moniker, Akbar the Great.

He commemorated a conquest, by building an elaborately designed entrance door to a mosque in Delhi and called it Buland Darwaza or "Door of Victory".

On the main gateway of this imposing monument, the first sentence, inscribed in Persian, reads "Jesus, son of Mary said: 'The world is a Bridge, pass over it, but build no houses upon it"

A bridge is a structure built to enable crossing from one place to another. Ever so often, one can take a little breather while crossing, a recess to stop and ponder but most certainly not to stay or hold on to.

As a past life regressionist, capturing myriad recollections of individuals from several lifetimes, I have observed that we, as humans, tend to hold on. Either to tangibles like personal property or to intangibles like pride and keep stalling our crossing over by binding ourselves to patterns of attachment.

As a speaker & behavioral trainer, here too, I see the chains of pattern in play. Many of us are persistently pleased to operate in primary performance styles and delay change.

And finally, as a coach, I have realized over the years that coaching skills are conditional, and clinging on to a set structure, staggers transformation for the novice to seasoned coach alike.

Turn to Google to ask, "how can I improve my coaching" and the engine topping result will proffer the standard "be agenda-less" or focus only on client agenda.

My dear reader, let us endeavor to break the mold here.

I say go in with an agenda. An agenda to raise the bar for oneself each time you speak to a client and all else will naturally follow. An agenda to get into a conversation with a singular objective to polish your techniques and power up your coaching prowess.

The development of ones coaching skills, I can humbly opine, is a bridge that one must continue to cross.

This is the genesis of the Principle of Auto-coaching.

Ever watched a Formula One car race on the prestigious Circuit de Monaco in Monte Carlo? To complete just one lap, a driver must make over 45 super quick gear shifts in about a minute and twenty seconds on a two-mile road. Multiply this by 78 laps and the number shoots up to an astounding 3500 plus gear shifts for the finish line. Auto- coaching, unlike a race lap, does not demand dizzying change. But it does require the mental pre-conditioning. In the racing rivalry movie 'Rush', the British champion James Hunt remarks, "The closer you are to death, the more alive you feel. It's a wonderful way to live. It's the only way to drive."

Metaphorically, as a coach, are you prepared to challenge your skill, ground it to death and evolve? Or at least try to.

What's in it for me, you may ask.

Population estimates peg the earth inching towards 8 billion of us. But we are yet to have 8 billion bestselling success stories. In the coaching world however, the competition scales down considerably. Searching online for the number of ICF certified coaches will reveal no more than twenty thousand. What separates you from the rest? Let's borrow 'learns' from our emperor; after all his rarefied clique runs into only a few hundreds.

Akbar, born of Islamic faith and reigning over a bellwether empire in the middle of the last millennium, advocated several unheard of and path breaking reforms. Amongst them, he called for a syncretic religion which entwined elements from multiple faiths and followed suit with the audacious courage to etch a Christian verse on his victory memorial.

Surely, he was pedestaled and pummeled in equal measure, but not for nothing did history ascribe upon him the sobriquet of Great. A Catalan Jesuit in describing Akbar wrote "his eyes were so bright and flashing that they seem like a sea shimmering in the sunlight". The oldest souls, I've noticed, possess this same shimmer. A life force emanates from them; a special energy that enlivens the lives of people around.

How do your clients feel about themselves when you coach them?

Have you truly experienced the joy of using your life force to cultivate your coaching style and in the bargain enable your clients to feel alive too?

Socrates' truism that "An unexamined life is not worth living" - begs consideration and let's look at how this maxim can unfold in your coaching practice by examining my own.

Retrospect - Introspect – Prospect

A few years ago, I took up a project to impart life skills to socioeconomically disadvantaged teenagers in the vicinity of my office. The plan was to train in a way that gently challenged them to open their minds and safely articulate thought streams while keeping the sessions fun and engaging. I decided to use drama intervention to involve the audience in evaluating & influencing emotional responses of the key players as the play coursed on. For example, in one act, the daughter of a street-side vegetable vendor proudly carries a successful school report card to her father who promptly admonishes her for disturbing him during a bad day and snatches the sheet to use it to wrap vegetables for an impatient customer while complaining about the cost of education. Our young audience lapped up the involvement with tears, laughter and realizations.

The method of Auto-coaching can be likened to a planned improvisation with you as the protagonist intelligently recording and directing your emotional and verbal responses.

I remember, early on in my coaching journey, grappling for responses to a dilemma presented by a client, much senior in age, experience and designation. In a hurried bid to bag his confidence, I found myself stumbling to piece together thoughts and asking suitable leading questions. I had struggled to manage both, emotional undulations and the resulting choice of words.

But it lit a spark. What would I do the next time around?

I grabbed a sheet of paper and replaying the conversation in my mind, jotted down instances of how I felt at various stages in the discussion and what I said in accordance. The ensuing reflections, I filled in a column labelled **Retrospect**.

On the next call, with the same client, determined to better, I referred to this first column and monitored my now contoured reactions- thought and speech- prudently capturing them under the neighboring column of **Introspect.**

It wasn't easy at first; I had to listen to two parties, the client and myself and equitably acknowledge both. Training myself on this multi-pronged effort needed speedily scribbled penmanship accompanied by sheer concentration and a vigorously chewed lower lip. But it wasn't until the third and final column came to life that I began to see the true advancement of this method and a brand-new way of looking at coaching. This third one, titled **Prospect,** saw me armor the column with a battlecard of takeaways to carry for the next session. Prior to starting the next call, I would quickly scan through this previous **Prospect** column and sum up instructions for me in a new sheet under **Retrospect**. And once the conversation began, I started chalking **Introspect** anew.

What I didn't anticipate was that I found myself glancing through **Prospect** columns of multiple clients to selectively pick an approach. Once the practice gained momentum, what hit me hard was that in focusing on shaping this process for me, my clients began to respond to the coaching with a stronger sense of profundity. I witnessed that even though my priority was self-construction, listening to their words with rapt attention became second nature. Both processes complemented each other. I was reminded of my daily evening drive home in peak Mumbai city traffic where one contends with potholed roads, zombie jaywalkers and a cacophony of honking vehicles adhering to zero lane discipline who sardine straddle your car. Yet drivers manage to unflinchingly videogame through this chaos while at the same time entertain an absolutely engaging conversation with a co-passenger. In the process of Retrospect, Introspect and Prospect (RIP), I meaningfully listened to & acknowledged client dilemmas while entertaining a conversation with myself. And all it took to ignite this was one sheet with 3 vertical columns and a horizontal line below demarcating the section for client comments. The inside joke is that I initially coined Prospect as Pain for pain points. Pain like Nataraja, a depiction of the Hindu god Shiva, is a multi-pronged progenitor. A worthy forebearer to the much-vaunted gain. And gain, I did and so did my clients. To a point where I use the sheets now while coaching all new clients and whenever else I find my mental mapping wanting.

If there's one thing that your clients will always remember and promote you by, more than any marketing or collateral or feasibility efforts, it is the continuous clearing of their mental fog. The RIP© sheets helped accomplish that by putting to rest my own dilemmas which gave me the courage to take on varied coaching disciplines and thereby truly widening my horizons. So, what can I suggest for yours?

Horizon Management

Recently, in a classroom teeming with trainers, I put up a picture of an outstretched sea with a ship centered in the distant horizon and a lone cloud sailing over it. I asked the participants to visualize themselves as primitive humans living on an island untouched by civilization and looking out at sea to one day discover this apparition. What followed was an intriguingly wonderful discussion on adult learning patterns on receiving new knowledge. And most captivating was what the natives did thereafter. As you progress through your coaching career, you will self-nurture with various tools and techniques. You will undoubtedly meet many coaches and will share and learn from each other. What I have provided here is a simple approach that worked for me. To quote MK Gandhi, a most loyal practitioner of his preaching's, "The best way to find yourself is to lose yourself in the service of others." Through the practice of auto-coaching, I was able to find myself and I hope it does the same for you.

Dexter J Rodrigues

Facilitator, Speaker and Coach for Corporates and Self-leadership,
Neuro-Linguistic Practitioner, Certified Past-Life Regression Therapist

Dexter is a facilitator, speaker and coach for corporate and self-leadership, credited with constructing creative learning solutions for an array of Fortune 500 clients.

As a training lead for over 15 years, he enjoys delivering sessions on mindset management for change and uses immersive learning techniques to skill build.

As a coach he has built a reputation for conducting impactful coaching clinics and works with leaders, entrepreneurs and support teams.

He has recently taken to regression therapy and has employed spiritual coaching within the personal and professional workspace.

He is a voracious reader, trained actor and enjoys scuba diving.

As the learning & development head at Datamatics Business Solutions Ltd, India he represents the organization globally and helps niche clients evolve their teams.

https://www.facebook.com/dexter.rodrigues

18

Reinventing Myself

BY SANKET PAI

Picture this! A shy, introverted and nerdy computer engineer frantically punching keys on his keyboard, working on ideas and models to create some of the best software for the best global companies. He has a proven track record for success and steadily climbs up the ladder of success to become the Head of Product and Customer Experience. He draws a handsome salary and fab benefits that put him in the top 0.03% of his demography.

One day he makes a transformational decision to listen to his gut and let go of his "safe" career. Well, that person was me and the transformational decision I took on a wintry December afternoon, about three years ago, was to pursue my calling to *"help people and facilitate making exponential changes in their personal and professional lives."*

I grew up in a middle-class family in Mumbai, and like most Indian kids, I spent all of my teenage and early adult years living with my parents. Growing up as a child, I was very fat. Other boys at school (I went to an all-boys school) used to make fun of me and my friends in the neighborhood used to tease me. I was subjected to body shaming. All this made me very conscious of myself and my body from the very beginning, and it gave birth to the reserved and introverted personality that I chose to box myself into. I went on to pursue my education and career in a field that complemented this personality. I even labored the goal of owning a software company for almost two decades, until one day, I painfully realized that I had been walking down the wrong path all along. In a 15+ year-long corporate career, I used to frequently have these little flashes - *"What the hell am I doing with my life?"* I always kept switching from one domain to another, one role to another, one company to another, one country to another, trying to find my sweet spot. *"Why am I doing what I am doing?"* The only answers I had were societal acceptance and financial security. I was so very seeking out the 'F' word widely used in the motivational speaking industry, which is fulfillment, but all I found was the other 'F' word - Frustration.

Soon after I took this leap, I realized I was swimming way out of my comfort zone. What I had missed entirely from the whole equation was 'people' and my apprehension to 'connect with them.' The intention to help and facilitate change was there, but I was allergic to using the key ingredient in the process. Fourteen months into the journey and I did not have a single paying client! A few pro bono coaching sessions happened once in a while, but nothing transformed into a paying coaching engagement. Over that period, I spent time getting my coaching certification, designing my website and writing my books. But that was just the easy stuff - I was still hiding behind my computer.

During this period I also spoke on a TEDx stage, and it was quite a story, considering I was a shy kid and I dreaded to stand in front of a group and speak in public. That was around the time I published my second book, 'Make It Happen', which is about nine people living their purpose. One of my cousins happened to share this with the organizing team at TEDx ICT Mumbai. The idea was to pick up a compelling story from my book and get the person behind it to speak at TEDx. But this did not materialize.

I remember having this awkward conversation with my wife, Kavita, and she persuaded me to step up to create the opportunity for me to speak on TEDx.

I was a certified coach then and had two books under my belt, and I still didn't believe in myself! However, after much persuasion, I committed to it, and as soon as the organizers agreed to have me on stage, I started getting the jitters as I'd never spoken on stage before. I realized that I had just committed to something that I didn't have the capability and confidence to see through. I knew I was scared and was feeling this knot in my stomach knowing that I was not good enough or capable enough for this talk. I struggled with this internal battle for a few days. Then, one day I had this flash of insight – one of my interviewers from the book had spoken about Dan Sullivan's 4 C's formula, which talks about going from a commitment to confidence through a process of four stages. It dawned on me that what I was experiencing at that moment was exactly this journey. It was necessary for me to feel that fear, and move through a period of courage to create the capabilities that were required. This realization spurred me into action, and I took up some Udemy courses on delivering TEDx style talks and presentations. As I went through the course, prepared my speech and started to practice it, I could feel myself getting into the groove, and finally became a TEDx speaker.

Things, however, did not change for me after this talk. After basking in the glory of a successful TEDx talk for a few days, I turned again to my coaching business only to see that there were still no clients. What was missing? It was very much my reluctance to connect with people. No matter how confident I appeared on the outside, the deepest truth is that I lived most of my life feeling self-conscious and powerless.

When the Student Is Ready, The Teacher Will Appear

The more I began to accept myself and release any judgments I held, the more I started to strip myself of my ego and see things through. The more I began to cultivate and strengthen my self-compassion, the more I began to foster a sense of self-acceptance. I realized that over this entire time of having no paying clients, I was discovering my strengths in having the tenacity and resolve and a commitment to achieving a breakthrough in the results I was seeking. In Dan Sullivan's words, *"A commitment requires selling yourself on doing something you don't yet have the capability to pull off."* This 'selling' for me includes knowing not only the WHAT but also the WHY. I attached myself to a bigger, better future - the one where I saw myself as a masterful coach working with extraordinary people to achieve 'impossible' goals. And it is because I want to make a massive impact elevating the lives of others while creating an authentic and abundant life for myself.

Armed with this commitment, I immersed myself in personal growth. As I invested in myself, I once again felt like a child - learning to flip around, learning to crawl, learning to sit up, and learning to walk - taking it one tiny step at a time. Quoting Bill Gates, *"Most people overestimate what they can do in one year and underestimate what they can do in ten years."* The tenacity and resolve within me gave rise to a period of courage to allow myself to jump to higher levels of capabilities and confidence. It also made me recognize that I had to get as much assistance as I possibly could. As I made myself more receptive to this perspective, teachers, mentors, opportunities, and experiences began appearing in my life.

Going forward, I would like to share three nuggets of wisdom that I learned from three of my mentors - John Assaraf, Michael Neill, and Steve Chandler. I believe these three nuggets would be of immense help, not just for any coach but also for every individual who wants to reinvent himself or herself to grow exponentially in their professional and personal lives.

Be Interested vs Be Committed

What's the difference, you'd ask me. I learned this from one of my mentors, John Assaraf, who is an entrepreneur, brain researcher, author, and CEO of NeuroGym. It's very subtle yet so profound that it changed my life and my coaching for the better. Quoting John, *"When you're interested, you do what's convenient; when you're committed, you do whatever it takes."* When you say you are interested in doing something, you will be sitting on the fence, you will have excuses when the going gets tough or even beforehand and you will procrastinate. You may also end up not doing that thing at all. On the other hand, when you are committed to something you will do everything in your power to make it happen. No matter what you want to do or what you want to accomplish, you'd certainly do it better if you are committed to it than just being interested in doing it. Commitment forced me into action, the very source of courage, and helped me move forward even when I was afraid of doing something. It taught me that the only way I can overcome fear is by doing what I fear.

Ask Anything from Anyone

The real fear I always had (and I still have it sometimes) when it comes to connecting with people is to ask them questions, or to be more specific, ask them for what I want. Whether it came from a sense of low self-worthiness or my inability to take a 'No' for an answer didn't really matter, because the resistance was there. The revelation came when I read Michael Neill's book, *"Supercoach,"* and I realized that my inability to take a 'No' stemmed from putting my self-image and self-esteem on the line. I was taking a 'No' so personally that I always made it about me, my existence, and my need for approval and acceptance. The book opened me up to a new way of seeing this. The premise is that a 'No' is never about you, even if the other person thinks it is and the moment you make it okay for the other person to say 'No,' you can pretty much ask anything from anyone. In other words, the moment you shift your focus from yourself to the person you're asking and turn your full light on how what you're asking will benefit that person, it becomes easy to ask for what you want. For me, this has helped me to make an offer to my clients and charge them for what feels good to me.

Set Yourself Free from 'I Gotta Be Me'

This one comes from Steve Chandler's book, *"Reinventing Yourself,"* and personally, it was a game-changer for me to get out of the mindset of *"I can't do this because I am an introvert."* I was always operating from a personality mask of a shy, reserved and introverted individual.

"This is how I am," I would say, and it soon became a common excuse for everything that remotely felt uncomfortable to deal with. In the book, Steve made an unusually blunt statement of fact, *"Personalities are not fun, vibrant things; they are what we crawl inside of to die."* It hit me hard. Our personalities freeze us into a stagnant pattern of being, and the moment we start relaxing the grip on this label, we can begin to see that we can become anyone we want to be. Being an introvert or an extrovert is no longer restricted to genetics or something that is etched in stone. This extrovert-introvert contrast isn't really a dichotomy, it is a spectrum, just like an amusement park roller coaster ride, which throws us into the extreme ends of the emotional spectrum and offers an overall exciting experience.

Confidence is a Result; Not a Requirement

After reading these three perspectives, you might still be thinking that one needs a certain level of confidence before trying out something new. You are not alone if you feel that way. It's a common myth that one needs confidence before attempting to do something new. I was lurking around this same myth when I started off as a coach. The truth is, to begin with, you don't even need courage or absolute clarity. All you need is solid commitment and candle-light clarity just enough to light a dog house. The commitment is what creates the necessary courage required to move forward and the candle-light clarity lights up just enough for you to see the next step consistently. Confidence then becomes an outcome of the thoughts we think and the actions we take. Circling back to Dan Sullivan's 4 C's formula, the fourth stage in the process is confidence - it is a result of the previous three steps, viz., commitment, courage, and capability.

Almost three years later, as I move ahead on this journey to help my clients see new perspectives, I am continuously climbing up the 'capability' ladder by investing in myself and learning new skills. I am exploring working with different types of people coming from different walks of life. Well, confidence is certainly a result, not a requirement.

My final two cents for any new coach or any person who wants to build a powerful legacy would be to keep reinventing themselves, to serve passionately, and do what their heart says. And more importantly, stay tenacious and resilient on the journey to glory. Be in it for the long haul.

Sanket Pai

Internationally Certified Leap Ahead & Human Potential Coach, NLP Coach Practitioner, EFT Practitioner, Author and TEDx speaker

My name is Sanket Pai and what I do is what I believe. What I see is that most people fear becoming irrelevant in their professional lives, but the truth is that they are just scratching the surface of the impact they could have. For some people, this fear may show up as a sense of inadequacy. For some it may show up as a struggle to tap into their full potential. For some others, this may show up as a fear of financial insecurity.  For some, it may be losing track or keeping up with the pace of their professions. For some others, this shows up as a feeling of not being there yet. For the remaining ones, this may show up as a state of feeling useless. Whatever labels they choose to put up, I help and support these individuals to reinvent themselves to grow exponentially in their work and also show up powerfully in other areas of their lives.

I am an internationally certified Leap Ahead & Human Potential Coach, NLP Coach Practitioner, EFT Practitioner, Author of 2 books - The Winning You and Make It Happen, and TEDx speaker. I live in Mumbai and Pune with my wife, Kavita, and daughter, Aahana. To find out more about me you can visit sanketpai.com or write to me at sanket@sanketpai.com

Facebook: https://www.facebook.com/leapaheadcoach/

19

Wedding SHAKTI:
The Secrets of Togetherness

BY SHRADHA WTB

'Wedding' has two meanings according to the Merriam-Webster's Dictionary. As a noun, it's "a marriage ceremony usually with its accompanying festivities" and as a verb, it's "an act, process, or instance of joining in close association". Shakti meaning 'Absolute Power' unites both, generating faith that's required for the process which isn't often apparent today.

I was born in a village in the by-lanes of Bihar in India. Sent to a boarding school at the age of four, I fell from the balancing-beam and fractured my shoulder in the first few weeks of learning to be on my own. My father's last words, "Believe in Yourself! Have Faith!" echoed through the eerie chilly woods of the Himalayas reminding me that soon sunshine would embark with his voice, fly past the nine months of rigorous training away from home and that was the prelude to my F.A.I.T.H. System that I developed over the years and now use to coach couples and individuals just like you to share the secrets of togetherness.

What is the F.A.I.T.H System?

A System is a way, a method of doing things. The F.A.I.T.H System has the acronym that stands for (F- Focus, A- Accountability, I- Invest, T- Thoughts, H- Hunger).

FOCUS: When you know why you want to marry, and whom you want to marry, the intent of the wedding remains intact and eliminates all distractions.

Focus on Friendship in the relationship. 1 out of 3 marriages fail in the first five years. 55% of the marriages that take place in the world today are arranged. People are marrying either under family pressure or just because the next thing to do after graduation and a job is to settle down and get married. Some even marry for sex. In countries like mine where more than 90% of marriages are arranged most people aren't taking enough time to say 'yes'.

What is your intent to marry? Getting to know your partner, sharing likes and dislikes, personal and professional goals are important to connect with them on an emotional level. The friendship you build during the wedding process is the baseline for the togetherness that is to last a lifetime.

ACCOUNTABILITY: A conscious decision to marry the chosen one, entitles you to take full responsibility to see the wedding through with self- awareness. *Hold yourself Accountable to respect your decision with Affection.* Mutual respect is the fundamental element of togetherness. According to the Oxford dictionary, respect is defined as, "A feeling of deep admiration for someone or something elicited by their abilities, qualities, or achievements."

What is your definition of respect? It is essential to integrate respect early in the relationship. Taking the time to listen, communicate and express freely helps you understand yourself and your partner better, offering space for both as and when required. It's absolutely imperative to observe and evaluate the experiences together.

INVEST: Time is all you have, invest it wisely to achieve couple goals together.

Invest in Intimacy to nurture the relationship. The Digital Age makes it even harder for couples to work on the varying types of intimacy that are important for the longevity of their relationship, apart from sexual intimacy (which is the common myth).

Physical intimacy enables you to show affection through physical touch and contact like holding each other's hands, hugging, kissing and cuddling.

Emotional intimacy enables you to share your desires confidently as the relationship evolves.

When brides and grooms experience spiritual intimacy they start sharing morals, values and ethics.

Intellectual intimacy helps you discuss important aspects of your wedding, like how to create a budget etc.

Experiential intimacy grows when you share your day- to- day experiences. Your relationship with parents, siblings, friends and anyone who matters helps your partner know you better as a person.

Conflict intimacy is achieved when couples break barriers to clear challenges; struggling but getting closer once the differences are resolved.

Creative intimacy keeps you in check - not to take each other for granted now that you're engaged; small gestures of love and appreciation amidst the confusion and chaos through the wedding planning process goes a long way in cementing the relationship.

Sexual intimacy, the most common one when experienced along with all the other types of intimacy, becomes truly fulfilling.

What are some areas you would like to explore with the one you wish to wed, but haven't yet because you let fear hold you back? Investing time in nourishing each type of intimacy ensures togetherness survives the test of time.

THOUGHTS: We have no control over the thoughts that enter us during the wedding planning process but we can choose the ones to dwell on.

Thoughts of a happy and successful married life helps surface love. Earl Nightingale said, 'We become what we think about'. The most important decision of your life, your wedding thrives on three main components; Life, Love and Longevity.

For a girl, she dreams of a fairy tale wedding straight out of a Hollywood or a Bollywood movie while a boy wishes for everything to go well and make all happy. Somehow in the process, often love is put aside and discrepancies take over. What began as a beautiful love story defying all odds that sent your hearts racing is now creating stressed thoughts of anxiety putting your mental health at stake. Weddings are highly-stressed emotional situations for just about everyone. What's supposed to be made in heaven, carries with it a whole lot of confusion, conflict and surprisingly chaotic situations that are hard to explain. To ensure your thoughts align with the core reason you said yes, take the time for mindful reflection; your core reason is the essential foundation for your togetherness.

What would your marriage look like 3/5/10 years from now? People who fail to plan, plan to fail. Most people have not planned enough, especially post- wedding, and they do not have enough drive and motivation to plan, much less take action. Visualising a successful married life enables you to plan for the big day and after.

HUNGER: The reason why you chose your life partner right at the very beginning holds more value than all the obstacles you face along the way of staying together.

Hunger to remain Honest to your Core. You were the one to say yes to your partner and the wedding and it's you who needs to participate in your own rescue. Most people wait for a situation and then decide to act upon it but those who are Hungry as my mentor Les Brown says, are the ones who prepare consistently, relentlessly and patiently to show more love. Work on your relationship, give it your all to live the best version of yourself. With faith in your heart, create opportunities even when you cannot find one, to surprise your partner with love, care and support. When the reason why you started the relationship remains priority it becomes easier to sail through the hullabaloo of the wedding process.

What is more important to you than the person you have chosen to spend the rest of your life with? Are the arrangements, the guest list and the extravaganza more valuable than your own state of mind? What comes first, family or career? It's all about increasing self- awareness and gaining perspective to love harder because where there is love, there is life and where there is life, there is longevity.

Who is a Wedding Coach?

The planning process of a wedding consumes our focus with such an elaborate essence of external details that the 'joining in close association' loses its sheen and is comfortably pushed aside only to create further stress and conflict. Brides and grooms face attention-anxiety and shy away from the turmoil in their minds, thus disconnecting from their partner especially on an emotionally charged day such as the big one that's got to be 'perfect'. A photographer, a DJ, maybe even a wedding planner are not enough. Fights about details that hadn't even occurred when you first got engaged, leave alone all the money talk deciding budgets, hit wedding nerves harder than anticipated.

A Wedding Coach is there for you! We help acknowledge that you and your partner's mental health comes first. With individual and relationship coaching for people who are planning to marry, targeted support around a huge life transition is offered that is judgement- free. You cannot see the picture when you're in the frame. Admitting a worry over your wellbeing through the wedding process is the first step to asking for help. With a little extra support over coaching sessions through The F.A.I.T.H System you will find answers to your anxiety that enable you to function with ease and calm in the run-up to your wedding.

Why did I develop the F.A.I.T.H System to Coach?

Faith can move mountains. It may sound cliched but whenever I met with challenges after recuperating on my own from that shoulder bone fracture I observed that it was faith that helped me dodge every curve ball that life threw at me. Whether it was raising my pre- mature baby or working in the scorching dessert amidst coal dust, or the rags to riches story of my short stint in the apparel industry, where I pulled a coup of sorts by registering sales of half a million US dollars in no time. After living like a dead soul in a moving body for several decades, my own Personal Development helped me go within to search for answers and all that echoed back to me was my father's words, "Believe in Yourself! Have Faith"!

A defining moment was in May of 2015 where I rediscovered the inner voice that had been submerged, suppressed and lost somewhere. The realisation and transformation helped me 'Witness The Breakthrough' which is also the name of my first book, an International Bestseller, with a foreword graciously written by the world- leading motivational speaker and my mentor Les Brown, the first ever for any Indian.

When people get curious about how to keep their faith intact amidst frustration I want to help them believe in themselves just as I did. I elevated faith to create the F.A.I.T.H system. I read somewhere, 'A good coach asks great questions.'

The F.A.I.T.H System provides a method to ask tailor- made, customised questions entering the mind, heart and soul of the client, and real transformation takes place.

How will people benefit from Wedding Coaching through the F.A.I.T.H System?

A wedding is the foundational structure to what lies ahead in a marriage. It is the best time to learn about each other and operate together as a team. The F.A.I.T.H System encourages you to look past all that weighs you down for whatever reasons, a System that compels you to hold on to that one thing, that one feeling that makes you want to love more over everything that made you upset and anxious for the silliest goof ups. Remembering to love your partner and being there for them through a sticky period is a skill that can be learnt and mastered with practice. Wedding coaching leverages the Power of Love through the F.A.I.T.H System as you approach the big day with:

- The Knowledge of how to deal with wedding anxiety through self- awareness;

- An Attitude towards parents/in-laws to align them with your 'wedding vision';

- A Skill Sets to stand up for yourself and your partner;

- Habits to communicate effectively with family, friends and vendors; and with

- Behaviour towards prioritising what's most important in the planning process of your wedding.

However, it takes two to tango, when brides and grooms both implement the F.A.I.T.H System consistently they experience togetherness that lasts a lifetime!!

Strengthen your resolve to love them more,

With each passing day, you will succeed,

Unfurl your thoughts, open the door,

Coaching insights, you can't on your own see!

Strengthen your resolve to love them more,

Share your heart with truth and clarity,

Coaches understand and care to listen,

Opening up removes all disparity!

Strengthen your resolve to love them more,

Break all shackles that are holding you back,

Confusion, conflict and hiding emotions,

Will only prove detrimental, creating slack!

Strengthen your resolve to love them more,

You'd be grateful, you didn't forever yelp,

Reach out, from your core,

Do not refrain from asking for help!

Shradha WTB

Wedding Shakti. The Secrets Of Togetherness. The F.A.I.T.H System
Speaker, Author, Coach Ambassador Les Brown Unlimited

Shradha went from being an abused and ridiculed "Fit for nothing," housewife for over two decades to becoming the most sought-after coach helping top CEO's, MD's and Country Heads, training groups at banks, hotels, universities and Fortune 500 companies.

Shradha became the first and the only Ambassador to the Les Brown Maximum Achievement Team, Shradha WTB is a Gold Certified Speaker, Trainer, Coach and International Bestselling Author, a pleasing personality and highly-sought-after resource in millennials who are in a relationship, just engaged or newlyweds looking to create longevity. For over two decades she has not only studied the science of love and togetherness, she's mastered it by interviewing hundreds of successful couples and observing them with proximity to understand their perspective translating theory into bottom-line results for her clients.

As a dynamic Keynote Speaker and leading authority on achievement for audiences that seek true love -Shradha WTB energizes couples to meet the challenges of their weddings, marriages and relationships.

With Wedding Shakti she helps brides and grooms gain clarity over chaos, putting their relationship in the forefront sharing the secrets of togetherness through her F.A.I.T.H System.

www.shradhawtb.com

https://www.linkedin.com/in/shradha-wtb-20b518111

20

"Everybody Is A Coach These Days."

BY MALEEKA T. HOLLAWAY

You may have read that in an article or on a social media post just as I did. At one point in time, I agreed with that statement. It did seem like everyone I knew magically became a life or business coach overnight. Having gone through a rigorous six-month certification process and another year of coaching refinement, I began seeing the coaching profession through a different lens.

While the work was fulfilling and often fun, it was still work. Being a coach was never fun and games; it was all about transforming lives. What I soon learned was that in coaching others, I'd be the main one undergoing the transformation.

When I first decided to become a certified life and business success coach, I had no idea of what I was doing. I knew that I wanted to help others break through the mental clutter that often creates a cushion for stagnation, but I didn't know exactly what a coaching practice based on that mission would look like for me. After earning my certification, for a strong year, I gave building my practice all I had. I attracted a large following online. I co-authored a few books, traveled the world with new friends and I found that helping others was a gift and a passion of mine.

But naturally, as time matures you and the path you thought you'd take changes, the next best question to ask yourself is "what's next?"

I loved coaching but I remember feeling burned out and wanting after each session. When a coaching period would end with a client, I often wondered what would become of them without me in their corner cheering them on? I wanted a way to continue the process that allowed for my clients to flourish without relying on me to guide them to making things happen. Eventually, I worked myself to a tizzy. And then, worked myself onto a new path.

Over time, I learned my place. I grew into my own coaching style. My reach grew and the people I attracted as clients proved to work out in my favor.

Here are ten lessons I learned as a coach and why I believe these lessons can help coaches learn how to function in their coaching capacity without getting flustered.

1.   Be coachable.

Every coach needs a coach. If you are a coach and you haven't had anyone as your coach since you earned your certification, that is a problem. To be the best coach you can be, having an active connection and coach relationship with another coach to help support you is necessary. Don't think you can grow and scale your business without help from an outside hand. To help your clients see success, you must also be invested in your own.

2.   Set your boundaries.

Every client is not your client. And every situation cannot be coached through by you. Learn your limits and boundaries and stick to them. Be upfront with your team and your clients. Set expectations about your working relationships and don't allow over-giving to become your default.

3. Know when a professional therapist or counselor is needed.

I once heard someone say, "I can't coach crazy." It was funny at the time but after delving into the mental health area, I can say I know what they mean. As a coach, you are not a licensed health professional. This means, you should not be diagnosing medical conditions or even insinuating that your clients should get checked for a condition. If you feel like you are not equipped to give the best support as a coach, don't be afraid to have an arsenal of professionals you can tag in when necessary.

4. Create an experience, not a transaction.

Your clients need to know that you are interested in their success, past collecting their payment. Even after their time is complete with you, don't be afraid to check in with them from time to time to see how they are doing. Offer a quick tip. Ask a necessary question and do it with no strings attached. It's much easier to earn the buy-in from previous clients who feel valued than new clients who haven't had time to experience working with you. Make your clients feel valued and appreciated. But more than this, make sure the work you do with them creates a memorable experience.

5. Learn how to unplug and refuel as needed.

Don't wait until you feel the burnout to step away. Don't wait until you start showing signs of being overwhelmed to take a step back. Make unplugging and recharging a part of your normal routine. It's not as hard as you may think. Taking an hour a day or one day a week to do what makes your soul happy is necessary. The work will be there when you return and you'll be better equipped to handle it.

6. Know that some clients may become friends but all friends won't become clients.

When you do good work, naturally, people will want to get to know you on a more personal level. Don't be afraid to let people in but be sure to protect your professional space. Creating great working relationships and experiences often lead to friendships. You never know who the universe is desiring to bring into your life in the form of a client. In addition, don't get upset when your friends hire someone to do something you feel you are qualified to do. Supporting a friend is one thing. Coaching a friend and getting paid for it is another.

7.   Know your worth and charge tax.

Your knowledge and expertise is valuable. And though you may believe it is priceless, in reality, it should come with a price tag. A good coach who can support their clients to achieve a desired result should be fully compensated. Don't think that you have to start low to build your business. It takes the same amount of concentration and energy to close a $100.00 client as it does to close a $10,000.00 client. The difference between the two is your mindset.

8.   Be okay with shifting your focus.

Time changes all things. You may start out coaching one group of clientele and look up and notice your client pool has evolved. Be okay with it. It takes a while to find your fit and to get comfortable. Don't fight the flow. Go with it.

9.   Be your own competition.

While it is good to know what's happening in your industry, it's even better to know how to stand out from the masses. Measure your success as a coach against your progress from the previous year. Don't look at external things to judge your journey. Embrace your process and establish yourself as your own measuring tool. This means you have to be in "go" mode and you can't let yourself off the hook to be "less than."

10.   Never settle for just being "good enough."

There is always room for more and for better. Face it. Even when you know you've done all that you could have as a coach and as a human being, there is always one more thing you could have done to seal the deal. Don't beat yourself up. Just get better. You didn't answer the call to coach just to be like every other coach. You chose to follow the path to make a difference in the lives of others. Own that mission. Own that charge. "Good" is never "good enough" when "greater" is still an option.

Maleeka T. Hollaway

Millennial business and Life success coach, Entrepreneur, Consultant, Speaker, and 3x Best-Selling Author

Maleeka T. Hollaway, a native of Atlanta, Ga, is a millennial business and life success coach, entrepreneur, consultant, speaker, and writer obsessed with personal development and small-business growth. A contributing writer to some of the world's largest publications (Business Insider, Forbes, Business.com and Entrepreneur), and a 3x best-selling author, her goal is to teach small-business owners and entrepreneurs to position themselves to grow sustainable and scalable businesses and brands. She holds a Bachelors and Masters degree from Alabama A & M University and is currently pursuing a Doctorate of Business Administration from Capella University. Connect with her on www.maleekahollaway.com.

21

Tether Yourself to Your Vision Pulling Yourself Through Uncertainty with a Vision That is so Clear That it Neutralizes Fear

By Kurt Wuerfele

"Make your vision so clear that your fears become irrelevant." - Anonymous

I wept with my face buried in my hands.

I sat on a rock in the middle of Flat Laurel Creek in Pisgah National Forest and grieved the loss of my dream that I had worked so hard for. After having been a successful business coach and consultant to insurance agents with the country's leading auto insurer, I had been promoted to being an agent myself, and moved with my family to the mountains of North Carolina. It only took a few short months to make me realize that I hated agency. I had a passion for helping professionals realize their greatest ambitions, but now I had moved from selling people on *their dreams* to selling them on car insurance, and my mind and body were paying the price. My moods would toggle from anxiety to depression; I started experiencing panic *and* anxiety attacks on a regular basis, and I disengaged in the life-giving hobbies and interests that had always given me joy.

In an effort to clear my head, to reconnect with who I was, and get a new vision for what was next in my career, I left for a week to backpack in the Rocky Mountains with one of my best friends. And this is where I realized that my experience hadn't been in vain; nor would it result in a dead-end. Rather, it provided clarity, and a new, clear vision of what should be. One night, over dinner, on the balcony of a 1920's lodge that overlooked Estes Park, I found myself coaching my friend. That evening, we *both* got clarity; my friend on his new career path, and myself on my purpose and path forward; I was going to become a professional coach.

In the following months, I struggled to find work in the mountains of North Carolina that would support not only my wife and seven-year-old daughter, but the very financial foundation I'd need to pursue my coaching certification. That year was extremely difficult, and although I was blessed enough to find consulting and training positions that utilized my skills with developing people, these opportunities were short-term, and engulfed in uncertainty.

I found that there was no amount of natural anti-stress supplements, CBD oil, or melatonin that could stop the dark cloud of anxiety that would haunt me throughout the day, and wake me up in the middle of the night in a state of panic...except for one thing:

A single, solid, repeatable process that I could follow that would keep me tethered to my vision, and the hope that I had in it.

It is a process that:

1. Creates a clear illustration of my vision;
2. Provides me with a record of my success which encourages daily action towards my goal despite fears and doubts;
3. Invokes faith by deliberately speaking and living out my new, desired reality;
4. Gives freedom from the initiative-seizing symptoms of perfectionism

5. Helps me to trust the process itself, and realize that I'm not making a mistake

As I progressed into my first three months of coach training at iPEC (the *Institute for Professional Excellence in Coaching*), I was even more clear on the fact that I had made the right choice. Not only was I excelling at successfully acquiring and coaching clients on weeknights and weekends, but I was also able to pay for half of my training tuition by month four. Not to mention, I was loving every single moment of this new experience. I had certainly found my calling.

And while the uncertainty of my main sources of income hadn't changed, here's what did: it was my ability to acquire coaching clients, to build my coaching practice, and to provide my clients with powerful and effective coaching.

I tell you this story because the road to *becoming* isn't an easy one, and you are seeing a lot of my personal struggles as you read this. However, I share this because I believe that I'm not a lot different than you, and it is my hope that through my experiences, ideas, observations, and learning, you will gain insights that you can employ in order to realize your own vision - even when things get difficult.

The following are the key examples of wisdom I've employed as I consistently walk towards my vision as it comes to fruition. These are some of the practices that have aided me in my efforts in overcoming the associated struggles that the accumulation of success will bring us all.

Illustrate Your Vision

A couple of months before I settled on moving forward with iPEC, I had reached out to a few of the other top coaching schools in the world and spoke with their admissions coaches as I gathered information on which program was going to be right for me. There was one particular admissions coach that I particularly connected with, and, with an incredible servant's heart, coached me for two hours. The vision she helped me generate for who I wanted to become and what I wanted my future as a professional coach to look like was so powerful, that I drew a picture of it so that I could make it even *more* clear. Around my drawing of my "future self," I wrote in the attributes that I most wanted to see within myself and in my future state. I've printed this picture out, and have put in in my journal, the home screen of my phone, and on my computer. I turn to this picture when I doubt and fear for my future. It not only reminds me of where I'm going, but in a lot of ways, who I *already* am.

Choose to be You, Despite Your Circumstance

It's inevitable. We're all going to have seasons on our way towards our goal where we feel dejected and hopeless. It's times like these when I've had to open my "progress journal" and read all of the weekly entries that I had made showing my accomplishments and the things in my life, collectively, that were going "right" because of the actions I had taken. This changes my mindset and reminds me of who I really am, because these were the actions and successes made by the man in my drawing; proof that not only was I becoming, but that I *already was* who I wanted to be, and that my situation will eventually change because of it. So, encouraged that everything I've been doing is not in vain, I press on, despite how I feel, with a drive to perform the business-building activities that I know will pay off now, and in the future. It helps to remember that all of the many great people who have ever accomplished their biggest dreams have all experienced this - it was simply their precondition to greatness.

Call Yourself a Coach and Live It

This was hard; especially in the beginning of my coach training. Our imposter syndrome sets in and wants to keep us "small and safe." But once I started telling people what I was doing, changed my LinkedIn profile to say "Coach," and found ways to serve people on LinkedIn from the perspective of a coach via quality content, the more I noticed something happening: opportunities to serve and coach paying clients started coming in. Old business colleagues, new professional contacts, members of former church fellowships, and acquaintances from around town started messaging me with questions. Some were just curious as to what I was up to. Others were excited and wanted to encourage. Some just needed to be encouraged. But all of this led to many asking, "can you help me? I'm stuck in my life/career/relationship/transition/work project and could use your guidance."

One of the most encouraging things that would happen to me would be when former co-workers of mine would ping me out of the blue after years of not speaking and say, "Hey Kurt! Guess what?! I'm getting certified to be a coach and it's life changing! Just wanted to let you know!" They were telling me they were becoming coaches themselves because they *saw me as a legitimate coach*, and were considering me a professional worthy of celebrating.

Boldly telling the world that I was a coach, even when I didn't quite believe it myself just yet, created the foundations of my new reality and truth; a new reality that I could start walking into and exploring. What I found was that others were more than happy to join me.

Anything Worth Doing is Worth...Screwing Up

This is some wisdom that I received from coach, Steve Chandler. I'm often paralyzed by perfectionism that is driven by an old script in my head that tells me, *"You're not enough. You're going to have to work five times harder at this than anybody else would, and even then, your best won't be enough..."* With this kind of self-inflicted mental abuse going on, it totally makes sense as to why I'd obsessively strive for stress and anxiety-inducing perfectionism; to the point where often times I'd quit before I even started. So now, I make it my aim to do my best and expect that something will get screwed up; maybe royally. At least this way, I can say I've moved forward, taken action, and called it "done." And *done* is better than *perfect*.

Trust the Process

As a professional guitar player, I've always admired Joe Walsh's electric guitar contributions to his band, The Eagles. One night as my wife and I were watching a documentary on his legendary band, Joe made an interesting observation. He spoke about how his experience with the band was much like life itself, where so often it appears to be nothing but anarchy and chaos; like a group of random events smashing into each other and causing all sorts of situations. However, when you look back on it years later, it appears as a "finely crafted novel."

I can relate to this, as my story sounds like this more often than I'd care to admit. However, per Joe's point, I can also see where there has been a common thread of inspiring and helping others towards their dreams; a trajectory of sorts, that I can honestly say shows that my journey is unfolding as it should, despite my insecurities and struggles.

Allowing myself to trust in the process that I am a part of has helped me to have compassion on myself and remember that my original vision and goal of being a coach was legitimate, and worthy of my relentless pursuit. And even if it doesn't look *exactly* the way I envisioned it, I've come too far, and have waited too long to *not* enjoy and rejoice in the manifestation of my calling.

Remember that as you progress towards your vision, no human being is immune to the challenges of "becoming." You will need to integrate your life and values into the desire for your vision and the path will never be straight, quick, or easy. It can take years for us to become smooth, much like a river rock that is slowly and gradually shaped by the sheer consistency of raging waters. You will never be the exception to this process...*never*.

If your vision is large enough, realize that it will never truly be accomplished, only fulfilled. But you can fulfill it every day. Make it a habit every day to take one step, no matter how small, towards your goal. And as you do, you too might just realize that you *already are* the person in *your* illustration of your future vision.

Kurt Wuerfele by:
10.01.21

Kurt Wuerfele

Professional Coach, Core Dynamics Leadership Development, Change Management, Trainer, Visioneering Guide

"Kurt Wuerfele is a professionally trained coach who helps successful professionals confidently reconnect with their purpose and reclaim the dream they once had for their lives. He has helped hundreds of people break through their self-limiting beliefs and find exponential success in business, life, and relationships.

Through his personal struggles and breakthroughs against fear, anxiety, and self-doubt, he has pioneered a path that allows him to guide his clients on their own journey of realizing their highest and most cherished dreams. He has since been on a quest to help as many professionals as possible discover who they were truly made to be and take hold of their lives with confidence in order to fulfill the vision of their best life. He has studied the craft of coaching under the industry experts at iPEC and the Energy Leadership coaching philosophies of Bruce D. Schneider.

When not coaching, Kurt can be found playing electric and steel guitar professionally, live and in the studio, backpacking, and spending time with friends and family. Kurt is a man of faith, a devoted husband, a loving father, and a guide to many. He lives in the mountains of western North Carolina in the beautiful town of Hendersonville with his wife Sirena, and daughter, Sadie Grace."

Email: kurt@lifepasscoaching.com
Website: www.lifepasscoaching.com
LinkedIn: https://www.linkedin.com/in/kurtwuerfele/
Instagram: https://www.instagram.com/kurtwuerfelelifepass/

BONUS CHAPTER 1
Why Coaches Fail

BY DIVYA LV JEGASUNDARAM

"The will to win, the desire to succeed, the urge to reach your full potential... these are the keys that will unlock the door to personal excellence." - Confucius

I started my coaching journey 6 years ago, when I made my transition from being in the corporate world of banking to being an entrepreneur. Having been in banking for over 13 years, I had the luxury of not having to explain what I do, where networking was easy and, acquiring new clients, as well as, growing the business and sales of my branch was pretty smooth going.

When I decided to leave my very successful banking career, the most obvious question from everyone was,

"What are you going to do now?"

My response: "I'm a Certified Life Coach and have my own Coaching Business."

In most cases, the reaction would be one of inquisitiveness, curiosity and skepticism, which often left me hearing myself justify my decision, along with fumbling with trying to explain the coaching profession, the role of a coach and the fact that I was neither a therapist, an advisor, nor an agony aunt or consultant. I quickly realised that if I wanted to help 'educate' the masses in this increasingly popular profession and be successful in this industry then I would need to be confident in my career decision, believe 100% in the profession and benefits of a coach and make a commitment to keep developing as a coach.

The day after gaining my certification I enrolled my first paying client, then another, a few days later, and another a few days after that and so it continued. Two weeks later I started as a lecturer for a leading international coaching school, teaching the syllabus and helping other professionals become certified Coaches. Over the years, while the main bulk of my business is Coaching, I also spend much of my time in training, consulting and particularly mentoring. As a mentor and coaches coach, I have been given a unique opportunity to help coaches build themselves and their businesses from day one of certification, thereby allowing me to work with them through their challenges and reduce or restrain that feeling of failing to be the best. So.... Why Do Coaches Fail?

1.   Lack of Confidence in themselves and the profession –

Many coaches struggle to confidently articulate what coaching is, their role as a coach and the positive impact of coaching to their clients.

Coaching will hit its peak around 2023; therefore, get comfortable with talking about your profession, and sometimes needing to explain more about how it works and its benefits. Use the experiences and successes you have had with your clients to give prospective ones a snapshot of the goals you help your clients achieve and the challenges you help them overcome.

To help build my confidence in the profession, I hired a Coach very early on. Five years as a lecturer and it continues to baffle me as I witness students wanting to be Coaches and yet never having undergone a coaching session or hiring a coach for themselves.

The next thing I did during my certification period was to conduct as many free coaching sessions as possible (97 hours in 6 months). This would keep me practicing, testing what I had learnt, gaining the confidence in my ability to coach clients to success, as well as developing my own style of how I would conduct my sessions. A lot of the coaches I see are not carving out time to practice and gain the experience of working with paid or free clients which perpetuates their (the coaches) feeling of not yet being 'ready.'

2. Pricing & Early Burnout –

Pricing – a topic that I have spent hours and hours discussing with many aspiring coaches. At one end I have witnessed charges as low as $10 USD/hour and at the other, $1100 USD/hour. Both equally shocked me.

Charging too little for your services will almost always lead you to be working with people who are not really your ideal clients, nor will you want to continue working with them as time goes on. Your own commitment level to your client will lessen as you start to feel undervalued, not to mention experiencing burnout.

Also, stop telling yourself that you are charging a low fee to build experience, and once done, you will increase it later. The 'later' doesn't come and instead you have created a market for yourself of low paying clientele.

Going to the other extreme of charging when you aren't ready to do so, will inevitably leave you endlessly searching for clients who can pay for your services, or finding yourself having to justify or defend why you think you are worth your fee.

Pricing yourself according to the market, your experience and your expertise will almost certainly secure you the clients you seek.

3. Be Selective –

When I tell my students or clients that they should be selective , I often get some odd looks followed by many questions that usually have to do with the fear of appearing to be a snob.

To be selective in choosing the clients you serve is to give yourself the best chance of staying committed, engaged, enthusiastic, and energetic with a genuine desire to coach your client to success whilst wanting to 'show up.'

What do I mean by 'show up?' It goes beyond calling or meeting your client at the decided time. To 'show up' is to be fully present in words, thoughts and actions.

Are the words I'm using resonating with the client, their goals, the purpose of why they have hired me? Are my thoughts on my client, on their journey, their goals, and their challenges?

Let me relate a personal experience I had with not being selective. It was just before I got certified and I was trying to work with as many people on as many different scenarios as possible. Eager to do gain experience and get hours meant that I wasn't selective in who I gave my time and energy to. Very quickly I found myself tuning out, or making fundamental coaching mistakes because I was being impatient, or getting frustrated with the inaction or lack of commitment from my client. Quite quickly, I realised this was happening because I lacked defining the types of clients I wanted to attract.

4.   Personal Development –

As coaches we use these words 'Personal Development' frequently. We talk of it, we promote it, we help our clients develop themselves, but somehow neglect to plan for our own development in the process.

Personal Development is most certainly a lifelong process in which we need to honestly assess ourselves, our qualities, beliefs, goals, thoughts and talents.

Start by asking yourself what you want more of? Or Less of? What do you want to start? What keeps you up at night? What is that nagging little voice of yours telling you that you need to do?

Regardless of age or life experience, self-development is a must if you are to grow as a coach. Just as you would upgrade your phone, TV or car, why not upgrade yourself too? What could you achieve or how would you be if you could be the latest version of you?

I can quite safely say that, coaches are failing in this area because they falsely believe they don't need to, so they don't make the time to invest in themselves because it's not a high enough priority for them. Make developing and upgrading yourself a priority. Coaches have goals and dreams as well. Coaches need to grow too. We don't have life figured out.

5.   Mindset –

As a lecturer, I always find myself talking about mindsets, coaching with a clear mind, keeping your attention wholly and fully on your client. However, maintaining the right mindset while coaching is always easier said than done. Often, coaches struggle with maintaining a clear mind, upholding a positive mindset, or stopping their mind from just wandering. We have gotten so used to being reactive to our phones, messages, social media or any other distraction that comes our way. We multitask in an effort to be more productive, yet we end up doing less, wasting more time and being dissatisfied with the results. Set yourself up with a successful mindset by having specific measures in place to help you declutter your mind and focus on the present. This could be as simple as scheduling enough time between client sessions, meditation, taking a walk, watching something that allows you to just relax your mind and thoughts. If you are to conduct fruitful, insightful, energising sessions you need to be able to focus entirely on you client, their needs and their life.

6.   Voice –

A pet peeve of mine is the quality of voice used by coaches. Your voice will either attract or irritate your client. As many coaches conduct their sessions in a non-face to face manner, it means that you cannot depend on body language or facial expressions to create the 'connect' with your client. The quality of your voice combined with energy and content will be the key to igniting that fire in your client to take action. Therefore paying attention to how you speak, what you say and how you sound will be key to attracting your client. An acronym that I coined for this is…

V - volume – how loud or soft you speak

0 - optimistic – how enthusiastic and positive you sound

I - intonation - the inflection, pitch, tone, rise and fall of your voice

C - choice of words – staying relatable and easy to understand

E - energetic – sounding upbeat and full of life

Whilst this last point seems like a very basic concept to be covering, it's a key lesson to take into consideration, as how you use your voice, and the quality of your voice can make or break your ability to gain rapport with you client paving the way to forming a lasting coaching relationship with them.

The 6 points that I have highlighted here are, in my experience, what I have seen coaches struggle with, which if not rectified leads them to feel like they are failing. The silver lining is that each of these points can be worked through with time, effort, persistence, patience, dedication, determination and most importantly the commitment to keep upgrading yourself and learning in the process.

As I was making my move into coaching, I remember reading the following quote by Steve Jobs that really resonated with me.

He said '*Your work is going to fill a large part of your life, and the only way to be truly satisfied is to do what you **believe is great work**. And the only way to do great work is to love what you do. If you haven't found it yet, keep looking and don't settle.*'

It's my belief, that if you are reading this book, then you are seeking to do more, to be more and to help others in the process, so follow your heart, let your intuition guide you and enjoy the journey.

BONUS CHAPTER 2
Coaching for Behavioral Change

BY MARSHALL GOLDSMITH

My mission is to help successful leaders achieve positive, long-term, measurable change in behavior: for themselves, their people and their teams. When the steps in the coaching process described below are followed, leaders almost always have a positive behavioral change – not as judged by themselves, but as judged by pre-selected, key stakeholders. This process has been used around the world with great success - by both external coaches and internal coaches[1].

Our "Pay for Results" Executive Coaching Process

Our coaching network (Stakeholder Centered Coaching) provides coaches for leaders from around the world. All of the coaches in our network use the same proven process. At the beginning of our coaching relationship, we get an agreement with our coaching clients and their managers on two key variables: 1) what are the key behaviors that will make the biggest positive change in increased leadership effectiveness and 2) who are the key stakeholders that can determine (twelve to eighteen months later) if these changes have occurred.

---

[1] **For a study on the effectiveness of this process with internal coaches in GE Financial Services, see "Leveraging HR: How to Develop Leaders in 'Real Time',** in *Human Resources in the 21st Century*, **M. Effron, R. Gandossy and M. Goldsmith, eds., Wiley, 2003.**

We then get paid only after our coaching clients have achieved positive change in key leadership behaviors – and become more effective leaders - as determined by their key stakeholders.

I believe that many leadership coaches are paid for the wrong reasons. Their income is largely a function of "How much do my clients *like me*?" and "How much *time* did I spend in coaching?" Neither of these is a good metric for achieving a positive, long-term change in behavior.

In terms of liking the coach - I have never seen a study that showed that clients' love of a coach was highly correlated with their change in behavior. In fact, if coaches become too concerned with being loved by their clients – they may not provide honest feedback when it is needed.

In terms of spending clients' time – my personal coaching clients are all executives whose decisions impact billions of dollars – their time is more valuable than mine. I try to spend *as little of their time as necessary* to achieve the desired results. The last thing they need is for me to waste their time!

Qualifying the Coaching Client:

Knowing When Behavioral Coaching Won't Help

Since we use a "pay only for results" coaching process, we have had to learn to *qualify* our coaching clients. This means that we only work with clients that we believe will greatly benefit from our coaching process.

We do not work with leaders who are not really motivated to change. Have you ever tried to change the behavior of a successful adult who had no interest in changing? How much luck did you have? Probably none! We only work with executives who are willing to make a sincere effort to change and who believe that this change will help them become better leaders. Our most successful coaching clients are executives who are committed to being great role models for leadership development and for living their company's values.

I have personally worked with several of the world's leading CEOs. One reason that they are so effective in leading people is that they are always trying to improve themselves – not just asking everyone else to improve. Our best coaching clients are dedicated to be great role models in consistently working to improve themselves.

Some large corporations "write people off". Rather than just fire them, they engage in a pseudo behavioral coaching process that is more "seek and destroy" than "help people get better". We only work with leaders that are seen as potentially having a great future in the corporation. We only work with people who will be given a fair chance by their management. We do not work with leaders who have been "written off" by senior management.

There are several different types of coaching. We only do behavioral coaching for successful executives – not strategic coaching, life planning, or organizational change. I have the highest respect for the coaches that do this kind of work. That is just not what our coaches do. Therefore, we *only* focus on changing leadership behavior. If our clients have other needs, we refer them to other coaches.

Finally, I would never choose to work with a client who has an integrity violation. We believe that people with integrity violations should be *fired,* not coached.

When will our approach to behavioral coaching work? If the client's issue is increasing leadership effectiveness, if the coaching clients are given a fair chance and they are motivated to improve, the process described in this article will almost always work. If these conditions do not exist, this process should not be used.

Involving Key Stakeholders

In my work as a behavioral coach, I have gone through three distinct phases.

In phase one – I believed that my clients would become better because of *me*. I thought that the coach was the key variable in behavioral change. I was wrong. We have published research on leadership development that involved input from over 86,000 respondents[2]. In our research we have learned that the key variable for successful change in leadership behavior is *not* the coach, teacher or advisor. The key variables that will determine long-term progress are the leaders being coached and their co-workers.

I learned this lesson in a very humbling way. The client that I spent the *most* amount of time with did not improve and I did not get paid! This was a painful reminder to me that I was not the key variable in my clients' improvement.

The client that I spent the *least* amount of time with improved more than anyone I had ever coached – and he was great to start with! He was later recognized as the CEO of the Year in the United States.

When I asked my 'most improved' client, what I could learn about coaching from him, he taught me a great lesson. He told me that I needed to: 1) pick the right clients and 2) keep the focus of my coaching on my clients and their teams (not my own ego and need to prove how smart I was).

In phase two – I spent most of my time focusing on my coaching clients. I slowly learned that a motivated, hard-working client was more important than a brilliant coach! I learned that *their* ongoing efforts meant more than *my* clever ideas. My results improved!

In phase three (where I am now) – I spend most of my time not with my coaching clients but with the key stakeholders around them. I focus on

---

[2] **"Leadership is a Contact Sport", H. Morgan and M. Goldsmith in** *Strategy+Business,* **Fall 2004 (re-published in Fall 2010 as one of nine outstanding articles in the history of the journal).**

helping my clients learn from everyone around them. By making this change, my clients' results have improved even more dramatically[3].

How do I involve key stakeholders? I ask *them* to help the person that I am coaching in four critically important ways:

1) *Let Go of The Past.* When we continually bring up the past, we demoralize the people who are trying to change. Whatever happened in the past - happened in the past. It cannot be changed. By focusing on a future that can be improved (as opposed to a past that cannot be), the key stakeholders can help my clients achieve positive change. (We call this process *feedforward,* instead of feedback[4]).

2) *Be Helpful and Supportive, Not Cynical, Sarcastic or Judgmental.* As part of our coaching process, my clients involve key co-workers and ask them for help. If my clients reach out to key stakeholders and feel punished for trying to improve, they will generally quit trying. I don't blame them! Why should any of us work hard to build relationships with people who won't give us a chance? If my clients' co-workers are helpful and supportive, my clients experience increased motivation and are much more likely to improve.

3) *Tell The Truth.* I do not want to work with a client, have him or her get a glowing report from key stakeholders, and later hear that one of the stakeholders said, "He didn't *really* get better, we just said that". This is not fair to my client, to the company or to me.

4) *Pick Something To Improve Yourself.* My clients are very open with key stakeholders about what they are going to change. As part

---

[3] **This process is explained in more detail in "Recruiting Supportive Coaches: A Key to Achieving Positive Behavioral Change" in *The Many Facets of Leadership*, M. Goldsmith, V. Govindarajan, B. Kaye and A. Vicere, eds., FT Prentice Hall, 2003.**
[4] **"Try Feed*forward*, instead of Feedback" originally published in *Leader to Leader, Summer 2002.***

of our process, our clients ask for ongoing suggestions. I also ask the stakeholders to pick something to improve in and to ask my client for suggestions. This makes the entire process "two-way" instead of "one way". It helps the stakeholders act as "fellow travelers" who are trying to improve, not "judges" who are pointing their fingers at my client. It also greatly expands the value gained by the corporation in the entire process[5]. In one of my most successful case studies, I was asked to coach one top executive – and about 200 people ended up improving.

Steps in the Leadership Coaching Process

The following steps describe the basics of our behavioral coaching process. Every coach in our network has to agree to implement the following steps. If the coach follow these basic steps, our clients almost always achieve positive change!

1) ***Involve The Leaders Being Coached In Determining The Desired Behavior In Their Leadership Roles.*** Leaders cannot be expected to change behavior if they don't have a clear understanding of what desired behavior looks like. The people that we coach (in agreement with their managers, if they are not the CEO) work with us to determine desired leadership behavior.

2) ***Involve The Leaders Being Coached In Determining Key Stakeholders.*** Not only do clients need to be clear on desired behaviors, they need to be clear (again in agreement with their managers, if they are not the CEO) on key stakeholders. There are two major reasons why people deny the validity of feedback - wrong items or wrong raters. By having our clients and their managers agree on the desired behaviors and key stakeholders in advance, we help ensure their "buy in" to the process.

---

[5] **For a great description of the impact of co-workers' focusing on their own improvement, read "Expanding the Value of Coaching: from the Leader to the Team to the Organization" in** *The Art and Practice of Leadership Coaching,* **H. Morgan, P. Harkins and M. Goldsmith, eds., Wiley, 2004.**

3) ***Collect Feedback.*** In my coaching practice, we personally interview all key stakeholders to get confidential feedback for our clients. The people who I am coaching are all CEOs or potential CEOs, and the company is making a real investment in their development. This more involved level of feedback is justified. However, at lower levels in the organization (that are more price sensitive), traditional 360° feedback can work very well. In either case, feedback is critical. It is impossible to get evaluated on changed behavior if there is not agreement on what behavior needs to be changed!

4) ***Reach Agreement On Key Behaviors For Change.*** As I have become more experienced, my approach has become simpler and more focused. I generally recommend picking only 1-3 key areas for behavioral change with each client. This helps ensure maximum attention to the most important behavior. My clients and their managers (unless my client is the CEO) agree upon the desired behavior for change. This ensures that I won't spend a year working with my clients and have their managers determine that we have worked on changing the wrong behavior!

5) ***Have The Coaching Clients Respond To Key Stakeholders.*** The person being reviewed should talk with each key stakeholder and collect additional "feed*forward*" suggestions on how to improve on the key areas targeted for improvement. In responding, the person being coached should keep the conversation positive, simple, and focused. When mistakes have been made in the past, it is generally a good idea to apologize and ask for help in changing in the future. I suggest that my clients *listen* to stakeholder suggestions and not *judge* the suggestions.

6) ***Review What Has Been Learned With Clients and Help Them Develop an Action Plan.*** As was stated earlier, my clients have to agree to the basic steps in our process. On the other hand, outside of the basic *steps*, all of the other ideas that I share with my clients are *suggestions*. I just ask them to listen to my ideas in the same

way they are listening to the ideas from their key stakeholders. I then ask them to come back with a plan of what *they* want to do. These plans need to come from them, not me. After reviewing their plans, I almost always encourage them to live up to their own commitments. I am much more of a facilitator than a judge. My job is to help great, highly motivated; executives get better at what *they* believe is most important – not to tell them what to change.

7) ***Develop An Ongoing Follow-up Process.*** Ongoing follow-up should be very efficient and focused. Questions like, "Based upon my behavior last month, what ideas do you have for me next month?" can keep a focus on the future. Within six months conduct a two-to-six item mini-survey with key stakeholders. They should be asked whether the person has become more or less effective in the areas targeted for improvement.

8) ***Review Results and Start Again.*** If the person being coached has taken the process seriously, stakeholders almost invariably report improvement. We then build on that success by repeating the process for the next 12 to 18 months. This type of follow-up will assure continued progress on initial goals and uncover additional areas for improvement. Stakeholders almost always appreciate follow-up. No one minds filling out a focused, two-to-six-item questionnaire if they see positive results. The person being coached will benefit from ongoing, targeted steps to improve performance.

9) ***End the Formal Coaching Process When Results Have Been Achieved.*** Our goal is not to create a dependency relationship between coach and client. While I almost always keep in touch with my coaching 'graduates' for the rest of their lives, we do not have an ongoing business relationship.

The Value of Behavioral Coaching for Executives

While behavioral coaching is only one branch in the coaching field, it is the most widely used type of coaching. Most requests for coaching involve behavioral change. While this process can be very meaningful and valuable for top executives, it can be just as useful for high-potential future leaders. These are the people who have great careers in front of them. Increasing effectiveness in leading people can have an even greater impact if it is a 20-year process, instead of a one-year program.

People often ask, "Can executives *really* change their behavior?" The answer is definitely yes. If they didn't change, we would never get paid (and we almost always get paid). At the top of major organizations even a small positive change in behavior can have a big impact. From an organizational perspective, the fact that the executive is trying to change leadership behavior (and is being a role model for personal development) may be even more important than what the executive is trying to change. One key message that I have given every CEO that I coach is "To help others develop – start with yourself."

References

[1] For a study on the effectiveness of this process with internal coaches in GE Financial Services, see "Leveraging HR: How to Develop Leaders in 'Real Time', in *Human Resources in the 21st Century,* M. Effron, R. Gandossy and M. Goldsmith, eds., Wiley, 2003.

[2] "Leadership is a Contact Sport", H. Morgan and M. Goldsmith in *strategy+business,* Fall 2004.

[3] This process is explained in more detail in "Recruiting Supportive Coaches: A Key to Achieving Positive Behavioral Change" in *The Many Facets of Leadership,* M. Goldsmith, V. Govindarajan, B. Kaye and A. Vicere, eds., FT Prentice Hall, 2003.

[4] "Try Feed*forward,* instead of Feedback" originally published in *Leader to Leader, Summer 2002.*

[5] For a great description of the impact of co-workers' focusing on their own improvement, read "Expanding the Value of Coaching: from the Leader to the Team to the Organization" in *The Art and Practice of Leadership Coaching,* H. Morgan, P. Harkins and M. Goldsmith, eds., Wiley, 2005.

Marshall Goldsmith

#1 Leadership Thinker, Exec Coach, New York Times Bestselling
Author, Dartmouth Tuck Professor Management Practice

Marshall Goldsmith is the only two-time winner of the Thinkers 50
Award for #1 Leadership Thinker in the World. He has been ranked as
the #1 Executive Coach in the World and a
Top Ten Business Thinker for the past eight
years. Dr. Goldsmith is the author of 36
books, including three New York Times
bestsellers, that have sold over 2.5 million
copies and been listed bestseller in 12
countries. His books, What Got You Here
Won't Get You There and Triggers have
been recognized by Amazon.com as two of
the Top 100 Leadership & Success Books Ever Written.

Linkedin – Facebook – Instagram – marshallgoldsmith

BONUS CHAPTER 3
Coaches Need Coaches

BY SNEHAL R. SINGH

Let's start with a quote by Bobby Knight. He says, "The key is not the will to win… everybody has that. It is the will to prepare to win that is important."

I totally believe that behind every fearless player, is a fearless coach; a coach who refuses to let the player be anything but the best he / she can be.

Professionally, I am a business coach and my major clients, truth be told, are life coaches. Thus far, I have trained and coached about 200 life coaches and having coached that many, I became curious and wanted to understand why coaches were hesitant to hire coaches for themselves. I mean, it is obvious that they have a passion to help everyone else, but why aren't they receptive to getting that help for themselves?

I am passionate about coaching and have unswerving belief in the impact of the coaching process. So, armed with this belief and my above-mentioned curiosity, I carried out a small survey on coaches. It was also done to crosscheck, verify, confirm, review…call it what you may, what I already had 'suspected' for a while. I wanted it disproved, but the numbers revealed otherwise.

Of about 160 certified life coaches who participated in the survey, only 70 of them actually had a coach for themselves. The remaining 90 did not, and probably didn't see a need for one. This, though not surprising, as I had been dealing directly with coaches for a while, was still puzzling and ironic….and disappointing.

If coaches are not hiring coaches, it is surprising that these very coaches expect to be hired. If you are a certified coach, I need not tell you the benefits and importance of having a coach, do I? Please, let me refresh your memory.

In my book, *I Work for Me,* I talked about the challenges I faced. I faced these challenges because I felt that I didn't have the required education or the right family background to start my business. Honestly, if I didn't have a coach to guide me at that time, I would still be living the same life, running the business from hand to mouth; the business would have simply been something surviving, not thriving as it is now.

I do not mean to imply that a coach did everything for you, but the coach challenged me, pushed me out of my comfort zone, and made me aware of my potentials and hidden talents. Looking back, I can see how much I have changed, and I am proud to say that a coach helped me…a coach coached me.

Having mentored about 200 life coaches specifically, and generally about 5,000 people in my entire career, and having many who still consider themselves my mentees even after seven to fifteen years, I am a strong supporter of how beneficial it is to have a mentor or to have a coach. I say this with conviction because I have personally seen the direct impact of coaching, both in businesses and in personal matters where you are heard, challenged and guided, ultimately reaching a 'good' place.

Coaches have the necessary and required experience to help you, offer emotional support, provide constructive feedback, and make themselves available when you need them the most, and that may be the best thing about having this relationship with a coach. You probably know this already but, based on the survey results, I think a good reminder is in line.

Being a business coach, I can assure you that the coaching business doesn't come easy. It is taxing and trying, so you need someone to guide you, someone you can talk to, and someone who helps you realize what the next step is. While I say this, my intent is not to scare you. I know that if you are a reader and are going through this book, you are looking forward to prospering in your business or prospering in your life. I know that you are trying to get to the next level of achievement. Instead of scaring you, I am just trying to alert you to the fact that the time is ripe to take the right action.

Coaching is a non-directive communication in which the coach prompts the reflection to release the activity to empower the coached to develop custom-based solutions for his or her problems. So let's find out if you need a coach by doing a little question and answer exercise.

So here goes!

- Is something urgent, compelling or exciting at stake in your life? Maybe a challenge, a goal or an opportunity?
- Is there an existing gap between knowledge, skills, confidence and resources in your life?
- Is there a desire within you to accelerate the results? Are you looking for faster growth in an area of your life?
- Do you feel a lack of clarity when it comes to making choices or decisions?
- Do you feel that success has started becoming problematic and doesn't come naturally anymore - that you are putting in more effort but yet remain uncertain if it is going in the right direction?
- Do you think work and life seems out of balance in your life?
- Do you feel you are creating unwanted consequences; do you feel like you are getting what you don't want?
- Do you feel it is time to reevaluate yourself and understand what your core strengths are and how you can best leverage them?

If you answered 'yes' to any of the above questions, then it is time to consider having a coach.

While there are difficulties in hiring a coach and you may get challenges like getting the right fit, (all of which will be talked about as we go on), let me first make it clear that you don't have to stick to one coach for life. You may be lucky, like me, to get a coach who is good for you and with whom you may stay for as long as you want. However, it is okay to switch coaches until you find the right one. You also have to realize and be open to the fact that, as a coach, people will do the same with you, as not everyone is the right fit for you.

Just because someone is a really great and famous coach doesn't automatically qualify him/her to be your coach. You are a unique individual and so you need someone who fits your unique life in terms of your belief system etc. Be ready to explore your options and get the right coach for you.

There are times when I get a question like, 'Snehal, what is the difference between a mentor and a coach?' or when I am asked which is better, a mentor or a coach, or when people ask me which of them they should hire, I tell them to get both. Coaching and mentoring are two different things altogether; they have two different manners of activity.

Some coaches look to hire a coach for themselves just so they can understand how coaching works. If you are looking for guidance, support and insights from someone who has already been there, where you hope to be someday, then you need a mentor and not a coach.

Whereas, if you need someone to stand in as an accountability partner in your journey towards your goals, if you need someone to help you discover which path you want to take, then a professional coach would be the ideal candidate to help you unlock that potential.

If you are still not sure if coaching or mentoring is what you need or you do not understand what the relationship with a coach would be like, then the following information will be quite helpful to you.

From the outset, you should know that professional coaching and mentoring, like other professional services, attracts a fee. Any professional coach or mentor has a pricing structure and should be clear about it, letting you know what you are committing to. Your commitment, however, is not just about the price of the program, but also about how much time you are prepared to commit to the coaching, mentoring and your own plans and goals.

Next you need to understand why you need a coach and why you should be committed to the program when you get one.

As a coach, a life coach or maybe a recently certified coach, what are your reasons for getting a coach? Are you looking for a coach just because you want to grow in the coaching business? Now, this is a prospect I honestly won't disagree with, as I had similar thoughts in 2014 and 2015!

As I was now a certified coach, everyone, including my instructor, kept talking about my need to get a coach. Hiring a coach would give me some answers on how to boost my coaching business. I would realize later, after going in circles, that, that was a false line of thought.

I kept going in circles because I played a stupid game where I'd get a client, then I'd try to help the client, then, being a new coach, I struggled with trying to use all the coaching skills I had recently learnt. I followed the 11 core competencies of coaching; not suggesting, not advising, etc. I kept trying to quote someone and I slipped many a time, going out of the realm of coaching . Gathering all the questions, I'd take them back to my coach asking for answers to prove if, or not, I did the right thing.

I soon realized, thankfully so, that all I was doing was taking a situation, trying to solve it on my own, then going to an expert and trying to grade myself by checking if I did right. I realized that it wasn't helping me and after a while I wasn't happy paying the fees. Looking back now, it is clear that neither the service nor the coach was the issue. It was me - I didn't have clarity as I wasn't sure why I needed a coach. I hired a coach because everyone said I should have one.

I didn't do my research on finding the right coach, or learning why I needed a coach. I just followed the logic that if I had been told to have a coach, I should have one. Hence my going around in circles.

I ended up hiring some coaches I didn't like eventually or having coaches who didn't meet my requirements because our belief systems, amongst other things, didn't match; but that is now water under the bridge as I have let those experiences go.

I am not saying that you will not make mistakes with a coach, neither am I saying that your judgment will fail you and lead you to getting a wrong coach. Instead I need you to realize that anytime we go through these phases, we, as coaches and individuals, are growing and getting more clarity in our lives; understanding ourselves better and knowing what we really want.

Let me share something about myself, something only those close to me might know. I am now sharing this because I feel it is important that you know this about me.

When I delved into coaching, I didn't have any intention of doing it full time. I was doing great as a certified behavior trainer and though I wasn't earning in millions, business was good. I was surviving; I was happy and I was content. The respect and connections I had established made me happy. The only reason I did a coaching certification course at that point was to upgrade myself, and earning a coaching certificate felt like the right thing to do.

I happily started on the journey of coaching simply because it was another certification that I could add to my portfolio and get a higher pay in future assignments - that was my goal.

I have never been one to think far ahead and then plan accordingly as I am more of a person who deep dives because it feels right at the moment and that was exactly what I was doing now.

It was then that the unraveling began and I became aware that this was probably what I was destined to do; that this was my calling. Coaching may or may not be for you, but if you picked up this book, then somewhere deep inside, you are looking for your growth, and I am addressing that aspect; the aspect of you looking for growth.

The reason why I am sharing these experiences in detail is to show how it has helped me be a better coach. These experiences have helped me understand certain things that I, as a coach should do, and having experienced them firsthand, learnt certain things I shouldn't do as a coach.

So will the process of finding and keeping a coach help you grow as a coach? Yes, it will.

Now, before you begin actively looking for a coach, be ready to invest in yourself. Let's go back to the survey.

One of the surprising answers I got from the survey on why those 90 coaches didn't hire a personal coach was that they felt it was expensive. It was surprising because if you as a coach expect people to pay you for your services, and are not ready to invest in yourself by paying another coach, do you really believe in the process of, importance of and need for coaching?

That is the big question.

If you do not, then you should put down this book and go find something else to do, something that motivates you. If you do not believe in the coaching process, it simply means that you do not really believe in your relevance as a coach! You should be doing something where you feel relevant. If you do not believe in coaching, then coaching is not for you.

Coaching is more than you coaching others, coaching is also about you being coachable. You have to be ready to listen and to be listened to. So if you are going to look for a coach, be ready to invest in yourself. Be ready to invest not just your time, but find some clarity, do your research and find out how much you can invest in yourself.

If you can't afford a coach for four sessions a month, maybe you can hire them for once a month. If that is still too much, get a coach who can coach you once in two months, although I won't recommend that much space between sessions. You would need someone to talk to, so it is always better to have someone rather than no one.

Before wanting to invest in yourself and before actively searching for a coach, there are few things you also need to ask yourself, such as;

1. What outcome, performance or improvement am I looking for? What results am I looking for in hiring a coach? What do I need help with? Which area of my life do I need help in? Such clarity is immeasurably important.

2. What am I ready to put in, to achieve these outcomes? What am I ready to do?

3. How am I going to manage my energy and time to put into practice all the changes that I would have identified during my coaching and mentoring? It is not just about hiring a coach, it is also about identifying things and then going back to implement and bringing in the changes that are required. So, ask yourself how you will manage that.

4. How will I ensure that my friends and relatives support me as I bring in those changes? Do I need to have a conversation with them? Do I need to tell people that I hired a coach, and so will be bringing certain changes into my life? You have to decide this personally as it is your call considering that you are the one in these relationships, and these are your people. You have to find a way to ensure that your friends and family support you to make the

changes you want, because your coach is not your only accountability partner, you need other people in your life to also hold you accountable.

5. What kind of budget do I really have? What am I ready to pay or invest today?

6. What kind of individual am I? What kind of coach do I need? Do I need someone with whom I'd like to have a face to face conversation or would emails be okay? Would a telephone conversation or would video-based conversations work? This is your delivery method.

Personally, I feel that the geographical location makes no difference and that is why I call myself the *Client without Borders Speaker.* I feel that it is all about having the relationship, having the individual, having a coach for yourself. I feel that it doesn't matter where they are from. I haven't done a single face to face session with any of my coaches. I like telephone conversations; I love video conversations because I don't have to worry where I have to go and I don't have to travel and incur avoidable expenses. I save money that way by simply doing a telephone communication and I'm okay with it, but that's just me.

You have to find your own way; find out what works for you. If you are someone who hasn't tried a telephone session at all, then consider having one to check if you like it. Try out a sample telephone session with one of the coaches. The key is to explore your options so you can find your preferences.

Let's move on to doing your research.

When doing your research, you should know that many coaches do ask for recommendations, so it is imperative that you answer the first question which is, '*What outcome am I looking for*' first, and find a coach in that genre.

If you are looking to upgrade or set up your business, you have to get a business coach. If you think that you are all over the place and you need a work-life balance or you think you basically need to find balance in your life before you move to upgrade your business, you should hire a life coach or hire a work-life balance coach. If you feel that you are great business wise, but everyone tells you that you are not good when it comes to relationships and it negatively impacts your business, then hire a relationship coach; find out what you need to work on, answer that first question first, then do your research.

There are three factors you need to consider while doing your research;

a. What has my coach achieved?

b. How can he/she help me?

c. Can I afford him / her?

You have to have these answers. You have to know how they can help you so that you can make the most out of the coaching sessions.

There are lists and websites where you can find coaches for yourself, so go ahead and do your research. Remember to ask your coach or mentor, whoever you want to hire, for details of their professional development; where they are coming from, where they have reached, and how long it took them?

It is okay to ask these questions to someone whom you think would want to coach you. It is not okay to completely depend on what the website says as it is necessary that you interact and ask these questions. Ask them about the credentials they hold, look at the coaches' or mentors' life experiences and how they incorporate them into their management, functional or business skills, psychology, sports, creative arts, corporate life or into their practice. Find out how their experiences are helping them.

Check their qualifications and experiences.

The most important thing is that you are satisfied that he / she is right for you to move you forward. You would want to avoid a situation where, after a few sessions, you go, 'Oh my, my coach is too new in this industry!' Do your research well , because the moment you have the belief that you have chosen the right person for you, the journey will be smoother.

According to Thomas G. Bandy, "Great coaches are visionaries. Great coaches instill, nurture and encourage vision, then model and motivate surrender to it." So, find that kind of coach, find yourself a great coach.

Once you have done your homework, make a decision. Reevaluate and then go ahead and take that step. Few other things to consider and be mindful about are;

- A coach is not to teach you how to coach, that is a job for a mentor or a teacher. If you are thinking that when you have a coach you'd expect them to help you coach, squash it. Also, when you have had enough experience of coaching and are ready to learn more, then go ahead and do the next level of coaching certification.
- A coach doesn't tell you how they became successful, except as their introduction. They help you find your own path to success. You don't have to do everything that they say they have done for their own success.
- The time to hire a coach is now, and not the day you become successful. You would want to have a coach now, to help you get there, wherever it is you want to reach.
- A coach should be hired because you want a transformation, transition, inspiration, strategy and many more things for yourself and your business, or for your personal and professional development.

I need to repeat that a coach is not to teach you how to coach and so if that is your purpose of hiring a coach, drop that idea now! If you want to hire a coach for your personal growth, then it is time to carry out the necessary research and get yourself a coach.

Even Bill Gates says that everyone needs a coach and that is true; each and every one of us needs a coach.

I hope this information helps you realize that as coaches, especially new or aspiring ones, it doesn't matter that you want to be or are in the coaching industry, each individual who wants to be successful needs a coach.

If you want to be successful as you grow, you should have a coach. Get yourself one.

WHO WANTS TO CREATE A BUSINESS THAT FLOURISHES?

"And the day came when the risk to remain tight in a bud was more painful that the risk it took to blossom." **Anaïs Nin**

For many Coaches, coaching is not just a mere hobby but a vocation and business. For a majority of Coaches, they haven't studied business and therefore often look for support and guidance on what to do from a business perspective. It conjures up a myriad of questions as to how best to achieve premium business targets. Targets such as; getting noticed on LinkedIn, constructing content, creating courses, developing websites, optimizing social media marketing, personal branding, speaking or, for some, even getting themselves certified as Coaches so that they can be taken seriously in this wonderful and varied profession.

Well…Guess what?

It is with great excitement that we decided to add a bonus section to this volume of Coach Wisdom! Here, we bring you industry experts that are sharing their own journeys with you. Our experts share their visions in order to aid you in your professional journey and inspire you to create the impact you need in order to generate and sustain a business that you can feel proud of. A business that you will not get bored of. A business where you can work smarter and not harder.

After Volume 1, we encouraged as much feedback from our readers as possible and then decided upon 7 specific areas we considered to be useful in aiding your fledgling businesses. As you read their chapters, we are confident you will understand for yourselves why these authors were chosen and the value that they will be able to add to you.

We once again thank our authors of this section, for joining us in our vision, for your energy, positivity and willingness to see beyond the norms of what a traditional book might be and stepping out of the box with us.

Divya and Snehal ☺

1

Look and Feel Fabulous at All Times

By Priya Rajiv

Is your image holding you back?

As Humans, the desire to look and feel good is a deeply ingrained trait. Dressing up and styling comes naturally to those who have been exposed to this intrinsic desire and made aware of its positive effect. For some of us, getting dressed can at times be a very stressful experience. A basic reason behind this is that most of us are under exposed and inexperienced as to what works and what doesn't.

The result of this is that we end up wearing something we are not comfortable with. A majority of the time we quickly regret our choices time and time again. This continuous dissatisfaction makes us fidgety and creates within us a stylistic self-consciousness and disconfidence, ultimately creating an emotional hole which seeps into other aspects of our lives. These emotional biproducts can be a huge deterrent in our success story because whether we like it or not, we are under constant scrutiny.

An individuals' image is a mental conception we have of that person. In a nutshell it includes your personal style, grooming, communication skills, poise and presence.

Does Dressing Up Stress You Out?

If the answer is YES! Trust me it's an easy fix provided you meet the right image consultant who works with and helps you build a wardrobe that not only depicts but resonates with the real you. Our aim is to give you the perfect cover for your brand story. We want to be that vital step that ultimately leads you on your personal quest to discover the best version of yourself thereby propelling you towards business and social success. All you need is some initial support and then you'll be all set to embark on your journey of success whilst wearing your unique SIGNATURE STYLE!!!

How Do You Start?

The 4 I's of Image: INTROSPECT, INVESTIGATE, IMAGINE AND INVEST.

Introspect-

Look deep within yourself. Find out who you really are and what you love wearing. Are you drawn towards simplicity, fashion trends, intricate detailing? Are you a classic dresser or comfort driven? Do you like attention and drama? Are you flamboyant? Once you decipher what you like the most, we can help you discover your unique Signature Style which in turn will be an extension of your own innate personality.

Investigate-

Become a wardrobe detective. Delve deep into your wardrobe and set aside a few garments. Identify the ones that you love and have received compliments whilst wearing them. Maybe it's the cut of the outfit or the color of the suit or the texture of the fabric that works for you. Stand in front of the mirror and analyze your body. Do you have more of straight lines or contoured lines? Keep in mind that you should always invest in fluid fabrics for contoured bodies and stiff fabrics for straight bodies. Understanding your body type will help you invest in the right garment. One that will immediately make you look fit, fabulous and fantastic!

Imagine –

You cannot create your perfect image without imagination! So open up those creative juices and imagine yourself in all your favorite colors. Think deep and explore that stylistic jungle! Why do you like them? Do those colors elevate your mood? Do you look younger? Does it bring out your inner glow? Does it make you stand out or does it make you blend in with the crowd? Color is the most potent means of communication. It can attract or distract. The right color can blend seamlessly into our very personas and create a rainbow of positivity. Therefore, choosing colors that work for you is extremely crucial. A wrong color can push you over the jaded precipice of tiredness and despondency.

Place your garment in front of you and stand in front of a mirror and blink.

The Blink Test: If your face stands out it means that you are wearing the right color. If your garment stands out it means you garment is overpowering, you. Remember the key to successful styling is for YOU to stand out.

Invest-

After introspectively investigating your imagination, it's time to invest! A small investment will make a huge difference. It will boost your confidence, improve your body language and your stage presence. Your clients will realize and respect your extra efforts thus valuing you more as a persona and a professional. Ultimately, a positive external image is a successful and powerful one. So spruce up your wardrobe, pick the right accessories and Dress for Success!

Why is dressing for success so relevant?

The environment and society we live in has a deep impact on our thinking and dressing. We mingle with fellow professionals, friends and family members who mostly set their standards by celebrity culture, social media, fashion blogs and general awareness. The need for constant stylistic appraisal and evolution is a vital social construct, especially for the young professional. It is a simple fact that the more visible we become the more scrutinized we will be.

Over time our job profiles, lifestyle and priorities will change as well as spending huge amounts on family, business, education etc. Like Hope at the bottom of Pandora's box, maintaining a positive image can be marginalized and taken for granted. Avoid this! Let your image exude confidence, self-love and success.

Know your why! Understand why it is important for you to dress smart and once you realize that dressing right is an important tool to propel your success, you will start enjoying the journey. Deduce what it is that is stopping you? Is it lack of time, energy, passion, interest or a fundamental lack of knowledge?

In Conclusion....

My message to all of you is please do not take yourselves for granted and do reach out to us. We're here to help you have a dream wardrobe that resonates with your dream role. Kick start your new story with a renewed energy and fall in love with the new you!

Start today.... INTROSPECT, INVESTIGATE, IMAGINE AND INVEST!!!

Priya Rajiv

Certified Image Consultant and Life Coach

Priya's foray into the world of image and style started in 1997 during her time at Lufthansa German Airlines as cabin crew. An extroverted and warm person, during her myriad travels, Priya discovered her genuine interest in helping people feel and look their best. While living in London she took her passion further by getting certified as an Image and Style consultant from London College of Fashion and Aston+Hayes London. Mentored by Jennifer Aston, one of the best in the Image Industry, Priya perfected the art of colour profiling and personal styling, making her a colour expert. Ever since, Priya has worked with numerous clients from various walks of life globally to design their personal  brands, enhance their success and discover signature styles that resonate with who they truly are.

Through this journey of inspiring, empowering and encouraging clients to step out of their comfort zone, Priya obtained her Coach Certification, where she was trained and mentored by Divya Jegasundaram. Priya uses coaching techniques to help clients live up to their potential by diving deep into their personalities, enabling them to revamp their image and helping them reignite their spirit, while embarking on a journey of transformation.

www.priyarajiv.in
Instagram - priya_rajiv16
YouTube -Inspire and Aspire
Facebook - Priya Mohan Rajiv
LinkedIn – Priya Rajiv Aiyar

2

Why a Quality Website is Essential

By Abida Noor

Why a Quality Website is Essential?

Here is why. A company website is not what it was 10 years ago. It is no longer a place where potential clients could go to learn more about the company, maybe post a question and possibly get a reply. Now however, a website is a centralized hub for all of the company's operations and functions. From a search engine optimized (SEO) e-commerce, to social media integration, a website collates all of these things into one place and serves as an integral part of the sales funnel. The good news is the website can still function as previously, featuring the company's history, FAQs and contact information, but more importantly it's the destination all online roads lead to.

Getting this right can be intimidating for a business owner, no matter how successful a business is or has the potential to be. Not all of us come equipped with the knowledge or technical ability required to create, let alone maintain this. Sadly, it's for this reason that many owners launching a new business neglect this crucial area. They may run their social media accounts well enough, being responsive to customer enquiries, and they may even be profitable without focusing on their website. But they may not reach the heights that they potentially could without an informative website.

The answer is to hire a qualified website designer as early as possible. This way a business owner can be on step ahead of their competition, who instead decided to go for a cheaper option in a short-sighted effort to save money. Hiring a first-class website designer isn't as expensive as one might imagine, and the rewards offered by taking this step usually eclipse what was spent anyway. A website designer will allow a new business the early tools it needs to be seen online and to generate enough leads to sustain it in that crucial first 12 months.

Benefits Of Hiring a Website Designer

The benefits of hiring a quality website designer are many. Not only does it allow the business owner to have control over their brand, but the website design will look more professional and customer friendly. Ideally it will also function this way too. Website designers are also well versed in SEO tools and this is will help generate leads, allowing the marketing budget to be allocated elsewhere.

Hiring a specialist website developer will also increase a websites security, stability and continuous optimization. For example, a developer will make sure that the website is created with a security certificate. This increases the likelihood of the website appear on Google or Bing's search functions and assures prospective customers that the website is safe and secure enough for them to add their contact details. If online transactions occur on the website, then this will make sure it's safe to do so.

Websites built on platforms like WordPress and similar models also come with many customizable options, plug-ins and updates. Having a dedicated website developer on hand helps navigate through this potential minefield and keeps the website functioning in the way it should, more importantly in a way that benefits the business.

Conclusion

The importance of building and maintaining a quality website in 2019 cannot be underestimated.

In 2019 a website of high quality is no longer optional but an absolute necessity for success in an increasingly digital age. This may be something that every business owner acknowledges, but simply acknowledging it is no longer enough. It needs to become a priority as early as possible for any new business. Today, a company's website represents the roots from which everything grows, and like a one-hundred-year-old bonsai tree, it needs to be planted and preened with near surgical care and precision.

One shouldn't trivialise the importance of hiring a specialist developer to build the platform and maintain it.

Abida Noor

Entrepreneur, Business Consultant, Web-Designer,
Owner & Founder of ServOn Digital Inc.

Our work is strategically organized, and customer focused in the most bespoke way possible to meet each client's needs and solve any challenges that arise. Our proposed Social Media Marketing Plan can be produced after our analysis of their present situation, offering our recommendations in a simple phased approach which also takes our clients preferences, brand and business model into consideration. The goal is to accelerate our client's marketing initiatives and boost their business revenue and growth.

We also offer business support to newly qualified coaches to launch their business by providing them with a vehicle that drives clients to them, making it a highly converting website. Many businesses fail to survive their first 12 months trading and we seek to fix this and help as many companies as possible.

Website: www.servondigital.ca

Email: info@servondigital.ca

Facebook & Instagram: @servondigital

3

It's A Calling, Not A Choice

BY ALEXA OLIVA

My company and I provide keynote speeches, training, and consulting services for businesses. However, my primary job is to book Bert Oliva, International Leadership and Human Behavior Expert, around the world in conferences as a professional keynote speaker and motivator. For many years people have asked us why we do what we do and the truth is; it really comes naturally from all the challenges, lessons, sacrifices and hard work we have put in.

Since I can remember, I think I have always understood that I have had an entrepreneurial mindset; I've always looked for opportunities that would provide a value to people. I believe that is why I fell in love with providing marketing and branding services for businesses. In fact, I went to school for it. I have a degree in Business and Marketing from the University of Miami.

For many years my husband Bert Oliva, and I ran a boutique-advertising agency in Miami. We serviced clients like Sony, HBO, Burger King, City of Sunny Isles, First National Bank of South Florida and many others. We loved developing creative impactful campaigns for global brands. It was a fabulous career and we were very successful at it.

But it was at this point in our lives that I became frustrated; every time we rolled out a campaign our clients would ask Bert do the presentation again and again. Our meetings were dragging on for hours because our clients just wanted to watch to him; they wanted to hear what he had to say. They were fascinated by the way that he presented his energy, his wisdom and then asked for his advice on their career, family, or business.

One day it dawned on me that we should monetize on the hours Bert was spending with these executives and business owners. I realized I could take my best product (Bert Oliva) and make it a brand. So, here began a lifelong journey of developing Bert Oliva into a teacher, mentor and international orator. We began this mission by attending comedy clubs in the late 80's so that he could study what they were doing on stage. We then began attending churches of every denomination to study the preachers and how they engaged their audience in their communities.

Soon Bert was being invited to speak at conferences and was paid an honorarium plus travel expenses. This is the point where we jumped from advertising to teaching about Leadership and Human Behavior.

The game changer was when Bert went to study at Xerox University in Leesburg, Virginia. There he was introduced to the godfathers of motivation. He learned from the greats like: Brain Tracy, Zig Ziglar, Jim Rohn, Tony Robbins, Omar Periu, and Les Brown. It was at that time that we decided to travel to meet them all and Bert was able to mentor under some of them, learn from them, befriend them, and even share the stage with some of them.

Part of this sabbatical we undertook was humbling because we carried suitcases, set up sales tables, sold tickets, hung banners; all to learn and understand what this industry was really about. We served to learn, we served to practice and we served to confirm our purpose. We finally understood that this type of speaking is a responsibility.

Speaking at a professional level is about bringing REAL VALUE into people's lives and into their businesses. This is not about ego; this is about truly serving a purpose with a strong message and delivering results. It is a message that is going to change people's lives; it's going to give them an experience or it's going to help their businesses truly grow. This is the main purpose of what we do and why we do it.

Today, we have spoken to hundreds of thousands of people worldwide. And by we I mean Bert, but I do get the opportunity to introduce him to the audiences and sometimes speak about what I love: marketing, branding, and video strategies. We still understand that it is an honor and a privilege to consult all these business and help individuals improve their overall performance.

One of the most important things that we have learned is to give back. I believe that when you get to a certain level of success, it is your obligation to give back. We do this by mentoring, coaching pro-bono or on sliding scales for some individuals that show us that they really want to succeed. We also make a major contribution to our world through Motivational Missions. This is a 501(C)3 non-profit, non-religious organization dedicated to social issues (e.g. Human Trafficking, Bullying and much more) that affect our communities and youth worldwide. What we provide are very specific entertaining and interactive assemblies in schools to teach Leadership, Self-Confidence and Empower our children and leaders of tomorrow.

Since the very beginning we have tried very hard to follow what we preach. And always take a hard look at our lives to make sure we teach what we have learned and what we have lived, but most of all what we believe in; balance. "Work Hard, Play Hard," has always hit a chord for both of us and thus balance has been pertinent to our lives. Through balance, we have been together and married for over 30 years, have raised our children and have the honor of earning a respectable living in this trade.

Over the past few decades we have met many people who want to speak for a living. But I believe to make an impact and a career from this you need:

1) Be dedicated to helping people with their issues or challenges.

2) Have a real certifiable message you developed with tools and techniques.

3) A passion for connecting with people.

4) A talent to deliver results.

5) A product or service that sets you apart from all the rest.

It really boils down to paying your dues and learning from the real professionals that have outlived all the fads and frenzies.

I will admit that during the hard and challenging times in this business I have wanted to quit, but then 'BAM' something happens to keep us in. After so many years of this, I realized and accepted that; It's A Calling, Not A Choice.

Alexa Oliva

Executive Director for BOWAworld and Producer
for BOWAstudios. International Speaker & Author

Alexa is the Executive Director for **BOWAworld** and Producer
for **BOWAstudios**.

She is also an international speaker and co-author. She provides key leadership and analytical support to major marketing efforts aimed at creating new revenue opportunities and improving current performance. Alexa is in charge of market research and product development, and has a strong strategic sensitivity, appreciation for innovative marketing solutions and respect for the "brand." She has an intimate  understanding of the structure of businesses and continuously develops better and more effective methods for product expediency as well as strategic development in the areas of brand development and video marketing.

Alexa has also been on the Board of Directors for the National Association of Women Business Owners, Global One, Mindbuzz Enterprises, Regional Policy Council for Miami Dade County, City Reach Ministries, FODS at Florida International University – Disability Resources Center and the Sr. Volunteer Coordinator for a 2004 U.S. Senatorial candidate.

4

Presentation, Prospecting & Profiting Using LinkedIn

BY RHONDA SHER

So many professionals are confused about LinkedIn. They still think of it as a place to look for a job or see it as a different version of Facebook. What they do not understand is that LinkedIn is a place to create valuable connections, develop a tribe of loyal followers, find new clients who want to invest in one's product or service and a place to get known as the expert in one's industry.

The first step to generating new business on LinkedIn is your presentation; LinkedIn profile. Many extremely qualified people have LinkedIn profiles that do not reflect their accomplishments. If you want to be taken seriously, you need to play the part.

Did you know that when someone Google's your name, there is a 70% or greater chance that you profile will show up on the first page of Google? Take a look at your profile. Would you do business with yourself based on how your LinkedIn profile appears to be?

Your LinkedIn profile should have a professional picture, strong headline and include an "About Section" that tells visitors what you do, who your ideal clients are, the product or services you provide, the results you get and how to contact you.

Your profile should highlight your work history, accomplishments, education and projects you have been involved with. It should also have several relevant and timely endorsements and recommendations. Bottom line, your LinkedIn profile should be written in a way that speaks to your ideal prospect or client to generate interest in the benefits that you have for them.

The second step is Prospecting. Prospecting on LinkedIn is not just hitting the connect button without a personalized message. It also is not putting a sales pitch in your connection request. That is the fastest way to lose a connection and a potential client.

Think of LinkedIn as a place to make real connections by getting to know people on a level that you would if you were off-line. Always personalize your invitation to connect. Tell your potential new connection what you have in common or why you want to connect with them, letting them know that you actually read their profile. Remember, it is NOT the quantity of connections, it is the quality.

When you receive confirmation that a connection request has been accepted, take the time to send a thank you message with a call to action. Again, this is not the time to make a sales pitch. Rather, it could be an opportunity to offer a free consultation to learn more about them and share a little about what you do. I like to make these calls a virtual cup of coffee in a "no sales zone". You would be amazed at what you can achieve by getting to know your connections on a more personal level. The easiest way to do this is to use a scheduling software and include a link to your calendar so that if your new connection wants to know more, you can easily set up a time to talk on the phone or via Zoom.

Another great way to stay top of mind with connections is to send personalized birthday and congratulation messages.

The third step is Profit – The way to generate business from LinkedIn is first by giving – whether that is sharing valuable content, giving a recommendation that has been earned, calling with a referral or simply showing genuine interest in your connections. Posting daily is one of the easiest ways to create a tribe of followers who not only read and like your posts, they share them with their followers.

Treat your inbox with respect. Respond to messages received in a timely manner. If you see a post that you think your followers might like, share it. Like and comment on other people's posts. Be someone who posts thought provoking, business relevant information that will make someone think or smile. Use hashtags in your posts.

LinkedIn is an amazing platform to find and create content and make meaningful connections. Take the time to learn how to use it.

If you are serious about wanting to book 2-10 appointments a week on LinkedIn with people who want to invest in your product or service, get Sales Navigator which is the paid version of LinkedIn and learn how to use it. Take the time to upgrade your profile or hire someone to do it for you.

Remember, if you are not LinkedIn, you might be left out.

Rhonda Sher

Lead Generation Expert, LinkedIn Speaker, Keynote Speaker

I Help Entrepreneurs Business Owners, Coaches, Speakers & Sales Professionals Generate 2 -10 appointments a week on LinkedIn - Done For You LinkedIn Profile Optimization - Coaching - Lead Generation - Keynote Speeches

To take advantage of a comprehensive LinkedIn audit of your profile on Zoom, the investment is $97.00 which is half price.

Payment can be made by going to Paypal.me/RhondaLSher

www.Rhondasher.com

RhondaLSher@Gmail.com

https://www.linkedin.com/in/rhondalsher/

5

Education is the Vehicle that Will Change the World

BY ZSUZSANNA KISVARDAI

A question that has always haunted me; "Who am I to do this?". I have always had audacious dreams which resulted in a great calling. "Visionary", they say nowadays; "Utopistic fool", they said back then.

I truly believe that education is the vehicle that will change the world. Not *industrialised* education, but self-induced, intrinsic motivation-led, and technology-rich learning experiences. This is why I created the *Teach Your Obvious* method. We can build an online academy, a "school in the cloud" as Sugata Mitra likes to call this.

I was born and raised in a developing country with 10 million citizens that has transitioned from hard-core socialism and very limited opportunities into a member state of the EU with the promise of freedom and innovation.

Yet only a few of us could live with the results this transition has brought about. And it comes down to two things; the lack of willingness to try new things and the lack of openness to new ways. Both of which comes with immense rewards in times of change. And I do believe that these qualities are crucial for entrepreneurship and coaching as well.

English is not my first language. We were taught Russian at school. But I wanted to learn English in a small, historic town in the north-east of Hungary close to the Ukrainian border. So my first teacher was an English teacher of Ukrainian origin, speaking no Hungarian, but fluent English. And my mother went over and beyond to pay for my tuition. And it paid off in less than a year when the teacher told me to apply for the special bilingual class launching the following September in the Secondary School in town.

"Who am I to do this?", I asked myself at the exam. But I was accepted. Strangely enough, my elementary school teacher doubted I would be able to get accepted. She asked me, "How come it is you and not the doctor's son who got in?"

You might not know that a socialist society is based on status earned by loyalty to the Socialist Party, not a trait that our family possessed. We were enemies of the system since my grandfather fought in the revolution in 1956. And in 1992, even after the change in political environment under the first democartic government, and still it holds after 30 years of socialism people have had bias with families like ours.

Soon after that, my parents got divorced and I had to work to support us. I was only 16, but I spoke English and back then it was something people paid decent money for. So I was contacted by the local community centre to teach English to adults.

Who am I to do this? Who am I in comparison to all those of stature? I kept dwelling on those thoughts over and over again. However, I had no choice but take the job as we needed the money. And I started to research the methodology of teaching foreign languages extensively. It brought about the opportunity to design corporate trainings to promote multicultural corporate culture.

Fast forward to my late 20s, my sister asked me, "Why don't you open your own language school? You've been running it for years for someone else?" I wondered again, "But who am I to do this?"

I opened my language school and made it profitable within 6 months. We served a very niche customer base; we taught English as a foreign language to very young learners. The amazing results we've delivered got us to the business growth that felt uneasy to manage. I was expecting my son and scaling my business in 2008.

Despite the recession, we were growing fast hiring people and I felt tired but on the top of the world. Suddenly at the end of 2009, I hit rock bottom. By Christmas that year, my business investor quit, my husband left us and half of my employees quit.

The question came up again. "Who am I to do this?" And in about 3 years my vision for an educational revolution became crystal clear.

We are more capable than we give ourselves the credit for. It's our responsibility to contribute to the collective intelligence by teaching our obvious without giving up on our personal goals. Serving the greater good is only worth if we as individuals grow from it. Yet it is scalable. So I am inviting you to join me in this mission.

There are a handful of online coaches and consultants who have already trusted me with turning their services into digital courses. And thus they've joined my mission to offer an alternative to institutionalised education, and archaic ways to distribute knowledge.

Some of these outstanding experts in their own field hired my *done-for-you* course creation service as they were caught in the rut of being overbooked by clients.

Others sought my guidance within a group of like-minded professionals like them building their own courses with my method, Teach Your Obvious. This group program has seen 3 cohorts so far, and I can't explain how grateful I am for their course launches and contributions to my mission.

In case you've been haunted by the 'Who am I to do this?' question, let me answer it for you. You are to do the exact thing that poses this question to you. Every time you feel the nudge to do something, listen in closely to hear if this question pops up. Then go and pursue that thing immediately after having heard this crippling question. I am with you in this.

Zsuzsanna Kisvardai

Online Course Creation Expert, helping you 'Teach Your Obvious'

I help to position your offer to become the 'top-of-mind' authority in your niche.

I have taught since I was 4. I slowly learnt that designing a learning environment is more important to engage your students than how much you know about your obvious.

First my teddies, then my classmates, and from my late teens, especially after university, I designed and taught a variety of curricula from English as a foreign language to special HR courses for multinational companies in Eastern Europe.

In a nutshell, I am an online course creation wizard who can design not only curriculum but can map out your student acquisition journey in a way that you learn a system, Teach Your Obvious.

Instagram - @ kisvardaizsu

Podcast - anchor.fm/teachyourobvious

6

Digital Marketing Controlling Your Online Narrative

BY SHREYA SHARMA

D o you wonder what 'digital marketing' actually means? Get in line with the two billion people asking the same question.

Many have an accurate impression of what traditional marketing looks like - TV ads, giant billboards, discount and sale signs on the windows of fashionable boutiques. This is because marketing has been around for more than a hundred years now.

However, digital marketing is still in its puberty (with the hard science being ten years old) and most people find themselves wondering exactly what kind of maturity will it achieve.

But there is a fundamental commonality:

It focuses on the *relationship* between your *brand* and your *audience.*

And the way they differ? It's that never before in the history of marketing has the customer had to opportunity to so proactively involved in shaping brand narratives.

Two words; social media. Every move a popular brand makes can earn it thousands of interactions on Facebook - likes, shares and comments. On sites such as Pinterest, the user-generated content *is* itself the product. You can't do that with a mail order catalogue or a billboard. In fact, businesses and professionals unfamiliar with digital marketing are often unaware that they have an online brand, but they do, and it is telling a story at all times. This actually mirrors a trend in real life.

When you look back and take a measure of your life, you see it as a series of milestones. However, when telling someone else about your life, rather than list those milestones, you narrate a story. The listener captures the distilled essence of your story. That distilled essence is an element of your brand as an individual.

So many of us, especially professionals, do not even realize we are unconsciously building our own brands when in fact we do it every day. We adorn our distilled stories in the form of clothes, music and friends, among other things - based on our self-image. That self-image is another element of your brand.

We communicate our brands almost unconsciously, as if it was an instinct. In fact, according to science, storytelling IS an instinct. Our brains are uniquely wired to forge neural networks via stories, rather than remember facts and details in isolation. We lower our guards, our skepticism and our logic when we're listening to what we identify as a narrative.

I've learned - as an engineer, a marketer and an entrepreneur, that even the most complex concepts are easier to understand if presented narratively. The big takeaway for brands - stories *inspire!* I probably wouldn't have become an engineer if Carl Sagan's Cosmos had not inspired scientist in me. I probably wouldn't have become a marketer if all the advertisements had not inspired emotion. I probably wouldn't have become an entrepreneur if our narrative of being one in our zeitgeist had not inspired me.

I bet that if you were to think about the moments of learning you've had, I guarantee you would think of them as narratives. And, as we've established, whether or not you are aware of it, your narratives *are* your brand. The whole purpose of digital marketing is to enable you to take control of your online brand, to take control of the way your online narrative. You see, building a brand isn't hard, nor is telling a story. You do it every day, even in a conversation. What's hard is taking control of that conversation online. At least, it's hard if you try to go about it entirely alone, making mistakes everyone else has made until you figure out how to do it right.

Two challenges confront us at this point. The first critical challenge is that a lot of brands don't even seem to realize that the customer has to be accounted for, to be given space to engage with the brand (and with each other). It's as if you were to give a speech and never take note of your audience's interaction. Absurd! That's how brands lose influence over their own brand's evolution, inevitably with disastrous consequences.

The second critical challenge is that the few brands that do realize the importance of accounting for the customer, don't realize that brand's owners themselves don't have to reinvent the methods and tools to make space for the customer. In fact, brand owners don't even have to learn the art and science of digital marketing. It's a strange thing, but a lot of them feel like that's what they have to do! That's like a customer at a restaurant feeling responsible for the way the chef prepares their meal. In fact, that's exactly why a lot of brand owners *do* find themselves intimidated by digital marketing.

In this analogy, I, and others like me - professional digital marketers - are the chef; you, and brand owners like you, are our patrons, for whom we customize and prepare the most delicious meal: a powerful customer-brand relationship.

Your responsibility? Focus on the brand narrative; audience, tone and image and effectively communicate your goals to us. It is my responsibility to worry about the data and the analytics, to manage the digital marketing channels and the associate tools. And when I say 'my', I really mean 'we', because the very nature of digital marketing means that its experts cannot work in isolation!

There are too many digital marketing channels for one person to master:

- *Content Marketing and E-mail.*
- *Web Design and User interface.*
- *Affiliate Marketing and Social media.*
- *Paid Advertising and Search engine optimization.*

Each of these channels come with its own tools, pros and cons. Digital marketing professionals tend to be *specialists*, experts in one specific aspect nurturing brand-audience relationships. It is fair to say that your biggest responsibility lies in choosing the right digital marketing partner!

- Pick a partner who values collaboration over competition.
- Pick a partner who is candid.
- Pick a partner who can manage risks and experiments.
- Pick a partner who educates and empowers you.
- Most importantly, avoid those who claim to be an authority in everything.

At Brandish, I help you control the narrative. I help bring people together for you.

Shreya Sharma

Founder – Get Brandish

Shreya Sharma is a brand communicator. When not making obscure and/or meta pop references, she helps small businesses and professionals tell their stories online. Her mission? To make digital marketing understandable and accessible instead of daunting.

She views life as a complex plot, with the Universe as narrator, and her own story as a (hopefully) fun spin-off. The chapters of her own life have spanned childhood in the Middle East, an Engineering degree from India, and a nation-hopping MBA through Sydney, Singapore & Dubai; until finally, she found a city that could keep her: Vancouver.

https://getbrandish.com/

shreya.apurv.sharma@gmail.com

LinkedIn - https://www.linkedin.com/in/shreyaapurvsharma/

7

Coach Certification
Choosing the Ideal Program

BY SUNIL LALA

Coaching is, undoubtedly, one of the fastest growing fields in the world. The demand for coaches both in the personal and corporate sectors – is huge and rising exponentially. If you are passionate about building a career where you can have a significant positive impact on people's lives, then the answer to the question "Should I explore coaching?" is quite simple. YES!

The devil lies in the details, therefore certain questions arise. Do I have the right qualifications to be a Coach? Where do I begin? How do I choose a great training program?

Let me get the most common myth out of the way first. You do not need a background in psychology to be a coach! In fact, you do not need any specific background. There are no pre-requisites to becoming a great coach and launching a successful coaching practice. So yes, you can be a coach!

With that myth out of the way, let us focus on what makes a great training program. With literally hundreds of coach training programs out there, the selection criteria can sometimes seem overwhelming.

Also, different people have different training needs. What might be an ideal program for one coach, might seem unsuitable to another.

Having said that, there are three important criteria that you should focus on:

1. Is it a high-quality program?

2. Is it convenient to attend?

3. Is it cost-effective?

Those are exactly the questions that we at Symbiosis Coaching asked when we were designing our programs. And based on our experience, here are some insights.

Quality – Highest ICF Standards

The International Coach Federation, or the ICF, has become the de-facto standard for Life Coach certification programs across the globe. Does that mean that a program that is not accredited by the ICF can never be a good program? Not at all. All it means is that pretty much everyone from individual clients seeking personal coaches to organizations seeking corporate coaches uses ICF as a basic metric of quality when hiring coaches. Hence, it is much easier to get your foot in the door if you have gone through an ICF accredited program than if you have not.

All our programs; Certified Life Coach, Certified Executive Coach, Certified Organizational Development Coach, and Certified NLP Coach Practitioner are fully accredited by the ICF, and recognized all over the world.

Quality – Highly Qualified Instructors

An ICF accreditation is quite meaningless if the instructors who are teaching that program are not qualified. It is, therefore, critical to look at instructor profiles. Are the instructors credentialed by the ICF? Are they practicing coaches? Do they encourage participation in class? Do they have the requisite communication skills that are essential to make a class engaging? Your instructors are your gateway to learning. Make sure that you are working with the best. At Symbiosis Coaching, we understand this, and ensure that we hire the very best coaches to teach our classes.

Quality – Support

So, the program you chose is accredited by the ICF, and the instructor profiles look pretty interesting as well. What about support? Is there a dedicated support team available to help you when you need it? At Symbiosis Coaching, our multi-faceted support system; Help Desk, WhatsApp groups, in-class support are all designed to provide our students with all the help they need, when they need it.

Convenience

If you are like most people who undergo coach training, you probably already have your hands full with everything else that is going on in your life. A career, a family, kids, elderly parents perhaps. Convenience is therefore a critical factor to consider.

So you must ensure that the program that you are considering is convenient. Do you have to physically travel to your class? Do you have to take time off from work? Or can you attend it from home? What happens if you miss a few classes? Are class recordings available for future reference?

Coaching is primarily an online field, and therefore, online coach certification programs are not just convenient, but essential to get comfortable with coaching format. Traditional programs offered in a brick-and-mortal classroom, not only require you to place your life on hold for the duration of the program, but also do not allow you a real-life coaching experience.

That is why at Symbiosis Coaching our focus is live, fully interactive online classes. These classes combine the best of both worlds – fully immersive, yet extremely convenient!

Affordability

When I look at the cost of some Coach certification programs out there, I cannot help but wonder - what were they thinking? Why would a six-month Life Coach certification program cost $2000.00, $5000.00 or $8000.00? That kind of cost doesn't make any sense.

You should not have to spend a fortune to get trained as a coach. In the end, all ICF accredited programs should cover the Core Coaching Competencies that the ICF has defined, and if they all do that, there is no reason for one program to cost $900.00 and another, $5000.00!

So why are some programs so expensive? I have spent countless hours thinking about this and have been able to come to only one conclusion; because they can get away with it!

Beware of all the marketing hype. A good, ICF accredited program, should never have a prohibitive cost associated with it.

We have priced our programs to be a fraction of the cost of other similar programs. We would rather enroll ten people who pay $900.00 each rather than two who pay $4500.00 each. And to make it even easier to enroll, installment payment options are available for all our programs.

Credential or not to Credential

Beware of organizations that promise you an ICF credential – ACC/PCC/MCC. No Coach training company in the world can get you an ICF credential – only the ICF can! And, while there is no doubt that getting an ICF credential adds tremendous value to you as a coach, applying for an ACC or a PCC is a very personal decision. Some certified coaches get an ICF credential, and others don't.

That is the reason, why we personalize our programs for you. If you wish to get an ACC or a PCC credential, look at our Platinum programs. Platinum programs include all three pre-requisites for an ICF credential, Training Hours, Coaching Hours, Mentoring Hours. If, on the other hand, you simply wish to get certified as a coach and start your coaching practice, just enroll in our regular programs and launch your career.

Business Building Resources

Check if your training company has any business-related support. That is something you will need to launch a successful coaching career. At Symbiosis Coaching, through Symbiosis Café, Art and Science of Coaching, and a library of business building tools, we ensure that you are ready to go as soon as you complete your certification program!

So, as you embark on this exciting journey, do keep these pointers in mind. A little bit of care upfront will save you a lot of heartache later on.

Sunil Lala

Founder & CEO – Symbiosis Coaching

After receiving his BS in Electrical and Electronics Engineering, Sunil went on to Boston University in Brussels for his master's in computer information systems. After spending a year in Europe, Sunil completed the program at the main BU campus in Boston and has been in Massachusetts ever since.

Sunil has worked in Corporate America for 25 years and has held various leadership and IT consulting positions in large companies such as Data General, National Grid, John Hancock, IDX and MIT Lincoln Labs.

As a personal passion, he has also completed his master's in biology at Harvard University, as well as his thesis on Merkel Cell Cancer at the world-renowned Dana Farber Cancer Institute. Sunil's passion for Life Coaching led him to become a Certified Career Coach. Realizing the huge and rapidly growing demand for Life Coaches in both the personal and corporate space, and a dearth of high-quality, cost effective Life Coach certification programs, Sunil launched Symbiosis Coaching with the goal of bringing ICF approved Life Coach training directly to people's homes.

Sunil's vision has made Symbiosis Coaching programs one of the most sought after in the world.

https://www.symbiosiscoaching.com/

Do you want to be in the next volume of Coach Wisdom?

Go to www.coachwisdombooks.com to find out more